TECHNICAL ANALYSIS
IN THE FX MARKETS

the technical *analyst*

TECHNICAL ANALYSIS IN THE FX MARKETS

DISCUSSIONS WITH MARKET ANALYSTS AND STRATEGISTS

The Technical Analyst Discussion Series

Copyright ©2010 Global Markets Media Ltd, publisher of The Technical Analyst magazine.

Published by:
Global Markets Media Ltd, 10 Quarry Street,
Guildford, GU1 3UY, UK
+44 (0) 1483 573150
www.technicalanalyst.co.uk

A CIP catalogue record for this book is available from the British Library.

ISBN 978-0-9564003-2-1

The author and publishers will be grateful for any information that will assist them in keeping future editions up to date. Although all reasonable care has been taken in the preparation of this book, neither the publishers nor the author can accept responsibility for any consequences arising from the use thereof or from the information contained therein.

Typeset in Times New Roman & Arial
Printed in the UK by MPG Biddles Ltd
Front and back cover photo: Getty Images and iStock

CONTENTS

TECHNICAL ANALYSIS IN THE FX MARKETS

INTRODUCTION

It is often said that most technical analysis methods are applicable to all asset classes. However, the foreign exchange market because of its size and depth undoubtedly requires a different approach. For example, a great deal of trading in currencies tends to be intra-day so shorter-term strategies predominate. Also, relative strength analysis (not to be confused with the RSI) that is used in the equity markets obviously has little value in the FX markets. Moreover, how to assimilate fundamental news into FX analysis takes on a different role; there are actually relatively few TA purists out there and as our interviews show, nearly all technical analysts pay some attention to fundamentals.

Meanwhile, the debate continues as to whether the depth and liquidity of the FX markets makes them less or more efficient than other asset classes. What is certain is that the FX markets are undoubtedly more technically 'driven' than other asset classes, whatever inefficiencies may exist. The findings of this book tend to suggest that inefficiencies do exist, but are short-lived and technical analysis is the most effective way of exploiting them, whatever particular techniques and strategies are employed.

The array of technical indicators available now can make it difficult for the analyst or trader to see the wood for the trees. While, the analysts interviewed in this book each employ a different approach in their work, ultimately they are all trying to do the same thing; measure market momentum, trends and sentiment etc. By bringing their views together, we hope to provide the reader with a clearer understanding of what analysts on trading floors around the world are actually using to analyze the global FX markets.

We would like to take this opportunity to thank all our contributors for their time, expertise and goodwill in making this book possible.

Matthew Clements
Editor
The Technical Analyst

May 2010

TECHNICAL ANALYSIS
IN THE FX MARKETS

Chapter 1

CHRISTIAN BENDIXEN
DIRECTOR OF TECHNCIAL RESEARCH
BAY CREST PARTNERS

Christian Bendixen joined Bay Crest Partners, an institutional broker-dealer based in New York City, in 2009. Previously, he was a senior technical strategist at Deutsche Bank where he was responsible for building the firm's technical research platform. He earlier worked for Bloomberg as a specialist focused on futures, options, and technical analysis.

USING TA FOR RESEARCH AND TRADING

Can you explain your basic research/trading style?

My approach to research and trading draws heavily on technical analysis incorporating top-down fundamental and quantitative analysis. I analyze the major fundamental trends that are driving global markets and then I overlay my shorter-term technical methodology to optimize my pricing for entering and exiting trades. I rarely initiate a position unless the fundamentals and technicals line up. I also use various price projection techniques to identify the risk/reward before initiating any positions.

Which markets do you cover?

I cover commodities, fixed income, equities, and FX. With regard to the FX markets, I focus on the DXY (Dollar Index), EUR/USD, USD/JPY, GBP/USD, USD/CHF, USD/CAD, AUD/USD, EUR/JPY, as well as some emerging market currencies such as the Brazilian Real (BRL).

How does your application of TA differ for short, medium and long-term time scales?

My application of TA does not differ that much for various time scales. For instance, I look for bullish/bearish divergences or negative/positive reversals using the Relative Strength Indicator (RSI) across most time frames. Obviously, a divergence on a weekly time frame has greater implications than on a 5 minute chart. It's also good to have an understanding how some of the more 'lagging' indicators such as the Moving Average Convergence Divergence (MACD) act on different time scales, obviously taking much longer to generate a buy signal on a daily chart than on a 60 minute chart.

I advocate looking at various time scales to ensure that they line up in the same direction. I have hundreds of charts and indicators that I divide into two groups - one group helps me track and analyze the fundamental and economic trends, while the other has all of my technical indicators/charts. Where applicable, I subdivide each group into long-term (~ >6 months), intermediate term (~1 month – 6 months), and short-term (< 1 month). Within each group, I break it down further; for instance, I will look at 15 and 30 minute charts to identify 1-2 day swing trading opportunities.

Do you think that the FX markets are more technically driven than other markets?

In my opinion, FX markets are much more technically driven than other markets. This explains why the trends are clearer and the charts look 'cleaner' more often than not. There is a lot more 'noise' in other markets.

As a matter of fact, I've reviewed academic research that concludes that technical analysis is a larger driver in FX markets than any other market, and FX professionals rely on technicals more than fundamentals and fund flows. I can't think of any other market where this is the case. Equities lie on the opposite side of the spectrum and they represent the least technically driven market in my opinion. Then again, and I may contradict myself here, I do believe that technicals for the most part are simply a reflection of fundamental trends, and technical moves happen for fundamental reasons.

How 'random' or efficient are the FX markets compared to the equity or fixed income markets?

Let me start off by saying that I disagree with the Efficient Market Hypothesis theory in general and that markets are far from being efficient or rational, and that's why technical analysis can provide you with an edge if applied correctly. In the markets, it's not uncommon to get a social contagion of emotions causing collective euphoria or fear, which is why it's imperative to study and be mindful of herding behavior.

Furthermore, there are so many fundamental cross-currents in the FX markets that I believe it's virtually impossible for this market to achieve high levels of efficiency. I'm not sure how 'random' or efficient the FX markets are when compared to other markets, but what I do know is that the FX markets are just as prone to collective euphoria or fear, which causes these markets to overshoot in both directions.

To what extent are the FX markets driven by sentiment? Is this possible to quantify?

I haven't found a reliable way to quantify this, but I strongly believe that the FX markets are driven by sentiment and crowd psychology to a large extent, which tends to be wrong at major turning points. I use market sentiment as a key indicator to determine whether to stay with my trade, exit my trade or take a contrarian trading position.

For example, in the fall of '09 a lot of technical signals started to line up suggesting that the downtrend in the US dollar was nearing exhaustion, including bullish divergences with several oscillators. When I saw how extreme the bearish sentiment readings were, it just made me that much more confident that we were close to seeing a reversal in trend. Given my belief that FX markets are driven by sentiment to a large extent, I think Elliott Wave theory works particularly well in these markets and it's a good tool to see how optimism and pessimism about market direction are reflected in waves.

What are the best sentiment indicators to use?

I usually keep an eye on volume and open interest to measure sentiment, and also to measure the 'strength' of an existing trend. Volume is impossible to measure accurately in the FX markets but one can overcome this by studying currency futures markets.

If you are not familiar with the futures markets, open interest is defined as the number of future contracts that have not been exercised, expired or unfilled by delivery. Volume is defined as the total number of contracts transacted on an average day. If the market is rising, you want to see volume and open interest rising together as confirmation that the trend is up and likely to continue.

I am a big fan of using the Commitment of Traders (COT) report that is published every Friday. This report measures the net long and short positions taken by traders in the futures markets, and you can see trends develop in speculative positions. I also analyze the Daily Sentiment Indices (DSI) for currencies, which give you a good sense of how extreme the sentiment has become in a particular direction. The DSI is published by Jake Bernstein and has been useful to me in timing the markets. Remember, however that contrarian signals can often be early so you have to use any sentiment indicator in conjunction with other techniques.

Are there any market conditions under which TA works better or worse than other times?

I don't think it's a matter of whether TA works better or worse in some market conditions than others. Over the years I've found that some technical methods work well in some market conditions all the time, all market conditions some of the time, but never all market conditions all of the time. Therefore, I think it's much more important to understand which technical methods/indicators to use for different market conditions.

Knowing where we are in the cycle has helped me identify when to use specific indicators. For instance, I will rely heavily on momentum indicators when I've identified that we are in the third leg of a move (impulse moves occur in 5 legs according to Elliott Wave theory), which is usually the largest and most powerful part of the trend. Along the same lines, its crucial to understand that conditions can remain overbought or oversold for longer than normal when we are in the middle of a major move.

INDICATORS AND STRATEGIES

Are there any indicators that work especially well in the FX markets?

Momentum indicators work particularly well in the FX markets, such as the Moving Average Convergence Divergence (MACD) indicator. It allows you to enter trades with price momentum on your side. The Relative Strength Index (RSI) also works well. I use it to spot bearish and bullish divergences between this oscillator and price. I also use it to spot positive and negative reversals. An example of a positive reversal is when the RSI declines more than price and makes a low below the previous pivot low on the RSI, but price stays above the previous pivot low. This is a bullish development for price.

I also like to monitor the various levels on RSI to identify how much room there is in the direction of a trend before we reach levels where we can expect a correction or consolidation. For instance, if the RSI is currently near the traditional overbought level of 70 but I know that over the last few weeks it has reached the more extreme level of 80 before reversing, I will stay with the trend and I will expect further upside in price.

What is your reaction when the charts show a very obvious technical pattern such as a head-and-shoulders or a double top?

I began my career trading currency futures where I was trained to identify trading patterns and apply a set of trading rules associated with each pattern. There are dozens of trading patterns that have a high success ratio such as pennant formations, but over the years the ones that worked consistently were the ones that weren't necessarily in the textbooks. I've also found that the most widely recognized trading patterns result in more failed trading signals. For that reason, when the charts show a very obvious technical pattern that is apparent to everyone I rely more on my other indicators to ensure that things line up.

I've found that most failed trading signals are very similar. Let me illustrate this with an example. Let's say you have a potential head-and-shoulders topping pattern developing and you then get a break below the neckline; what usually happens is that you get a very fast move to the downside because new positions are being entered on the break and because a number of stop levels are being triggered given that the neckline was also a support level and stops were entered just below that support level for long positions. For a little while it may appear that the pattern is fulfilling its implications, but sometimes you get an exhaustion of sellers after the stops get triggered and you get a snap move back above the neckline, at which point shorts get nervous and may start covering some of their positions, and it becomes a failed breakdown.

One more comment I want to make. I've found that failed trading patterns can often become the best and most reliable patterns. In other words, if you see a failed head-and-shoulders pattern and a break back above the neckline, it's often an opportune time to get long, especially after it breaks above the previous right shoulder.

How do you identify when a trend has commenced and may be nearing its end?

Firstly, I try to identify trends that are displaying signs of 'trend exhaustion'. I rely on bearish and bullish divergences between oscillators and price for that purpose, with the understanding that divergences usually take a long time to play out. Then, I use a combination of Elliott Wave and Gann techniques to identify a confluence of potential inflection points. I also use trendlines and Gann lines to identify the beginning of a new trend, while also relying on moving averages, especially exponential moving averages and crossovers of those moving averages to confirm a new trend. Furthermore, I believe that RSI has a tendency to lead price, so if RSI breaks a trendline there is a high likelihood that price will soon follow.

I used some of these methods to indentify the exhaustion of the downtrend in the US dollar and the uptrend in the Euro in late '09, when I entered into a structural long on the USD and a structural short on the Euro. The charts I've included below were taken from a report I wrote on December 9th 2009. Figure 1 is a daily chart of the US dollar, which illustrates how I spotted a major bullish divergence with the RSI, and how it broke out of a trendline before price did, in addition to a completed Elliott Wave pattern.

Figure 2 is a weekly chart showing a 'momentum' buy signal as well as the RSI bouncing off the traditional 30 oversold level. Figure 3 is a daily chart showing how the Euro failed at the last Fibonacci retracement level in addition to showing a bearish divergence with RSI.

What period do you use for the RSI and why?

I use several different periods for RSI depending on the time frame that I want to analyze but the one that has proven to be the most reliable for me is the 21 periodicity. I have found that reversals from the different levels are more reliable using this periodicity, and more consistent. I also use the periods of 9 and 14.

What is the best method for measuring price momentum in the market?

I use the Relative Strength Index (RSI), the Moving Average Convergence Divergence (MACD), and the price Rate of Change (ROC), to measure the momentum of a currency's trend and the likelihood that it will continue.

Many of these momentum indicators are bound between two extreme levels, usually 0 to 100 or -100 to +100. This is important because a cross through the center line of the indicator suggests that momentum is either increasing or decreasing, depending on the direction. For example, momentum is said to be increasing when the ROC indicator crosses above the 0 line, and decreasing when it crosses down through 0.

Do you use Fibonacci, Gann or Elliott Wave techniques and if so, how?

I use all of those techniques extensively. I've always believed that its not enough to identify trading setups based on price alone, and that's why I rely on Gann to identify 'time' setups. I'm also a big fan of using Gann Angles (using geometric angles is an important part of the Gann trading method). These angles offer us price levels that move with time. Gann believed that the markets are geometric in design and function. For example, the 45 degree angle line is usually referred to as the "1x1" angle, because it represents one unit of price with one unit of time. I use these Gann lines to help me show where there is support and resistance, and they also have predictive value for future direction and price activity to help me forecast where the market may be and when it is likely to get there. Combining time analysis with price analysis has been an important element of my approach to research/trading.

I use Fibonacci extensions and retracement levels to identify potential price targets. Fibonacci is also helpful in identifying various price relationships between different legs in a wave structure. For instance, the third leg is usually a Fibonacci extension of the first leg.

Also, I look at Elliott Wave techniques to identify trends and countertrends, trend continuation or exhaustion, and to evaluate potential price targets of a trend. I believe that the markets move in a repetitive pattern and that fractals are abundant – in other words, you can see the same patterns appearing on several time frames.

An impulse wave in the direction of the trend occurs in 5 waves. I have developed techniques and indicators that try and help me identify and capture the 3rd wave, which is usually the longest and most powerful part of a move. This trend usually starts slowly, but tends to accelerate as it breaks to new highs above the top of Wave 1 if we are in an uptrend. Sometimes, I also try and capture the 5th leg. A recent example of this was with the Euro (Figure 4). It underwent a long consolidation period but failed to overcome the 50-day moving average, and it appeared that we had only moved up in a three leg corrective pattern, so the odds were high that we still had at least another leg lower. Furthermore, if I've identified the 5th leg, I will look for divergences with my oscillators to try and position myself for a trend reversal.

Which Fibonacci percentage do you think is the most reliable?

The most reliable Fib percentages for me have been 38.2% and the 61.8%. Depending on where you are in the 'cycle' you can assign different probabilities to different Fib levels. For instance, if you are in an uptrend, and you think you are retracing to complete a leg 2 correction, then more often than not, you retrace a large part of the initial impulsive leg 1. So in most leg 2s you will retrace to the 61.8% retracement level. If, on the other hand, you are in a leg 3 and you are in the middle of a strong uptrend, more likely than not, you will just retrace 38.2%. The most reliable Fibonacci extension levels for me have been 1.382 and 1.618.

How do you use moving averages? If so, which periodicities do you use and do you use them directly to generate trade signals?

While I do use simple moving averages such as the 50-day and the 200-day, I tend to gravitate more towards exponential moving averages which work better in my opinion. I use moving averages for resistance and support levels, and I use the crossovers of moving averages for 'buy' and 'sell' signals. The one that has worked the best for me is applying the 20, 35, and 50 exponential moving averages together on the same chart and using the triple crossover of these averages as buy and sell signals (Figure 1).

If prices reach a major support level do you wait until it has broken through before buying or selling?

Nowadays, failed breakouts and breakdowns occur so frequently that I try to anticipate a break of a major support level instead of waiting for that level to be broken, and I usually initiate a trade/position near another pivot level so that the risk/reward is compelling.

How do you judge if a market is overbought or oversold?

I rely heavily on the RSI to determine if a market is overbought or oversold. While most people use the default settings for the overbought and oversold levels, I think it's important to look at the historical RSI action to determine which level has acted as resistance or support for the RSI and use those levels. In addition its important to understand that in an uptrend (i.e. cyclical bull market) the RSI usually goes up to 80-85 whereas in a downtrend (i.e. cyclical bear market) it usually fails at 60-65, so you have to adjust the levels you use to understand if it is overbought or oversold.

CHARACTERISTICS UNIQUE TO THE FX MARKETS

How far out do you analyze the FX markets? What specific strategies do you use for longer-term analysis?

I do use longer-term monthly charts and Elliott Wave and Gann techniques to forecast out longer than 6 months but my focus is on the shorter-term. However, it is important to be mindful of what the longer-term cycles and trends are telling you.

Is there any difference in your approach between the analysis of G7 and emerging markets currencies? To what extent is liquidity in EM markets a factor?

There is no difference in my approach but some EM currencies have a tendency to be more volatile, so I use the techniques described above to determine how much more volatile the currency is and then I adjust my parameters accordingly. Liquidity risk is always a concern when trading EM currencies, so one needs to take that extra risk into consideration when trading these currencies.

To what extent do you look at fundamental information?

I believe that fundamentals are the primary drivers of market direction and prices, so I think it's imperative to understand the fundamental picture. Once I have a good understanding of the major fundamental trends, I then move on towards analyzing the technical picture.

What fundamental information is most important for the FX markets?

The challenge when analyzing the FX markets is the vast amount of fundamental information that one needs to peruse through. Lots of factors influence currencies but most are either political or economic. The level of interest rates is a major factor in the strength or weakness of a currency. High rates have generally boosted a currency's value. This is most likely due to the carry trade which sees speculators borrow money in a low-yielding currency and then invest the proceeds in a higher-yielding one

It's important to have a good understanding of the country's fiscal situation and monetary policy. The health of the economy is important as well and often determines the interest rate differential between two countries. For instance, I am currently arguing that economic conditions are improving more rapidly in the US than in Europe and so it is more likely that the US will raise rates sooner than Europe and if that's the case, the USD should continue to move higher over the intermediate term. Longer-term, the fiscal situation in the US is deteriorating with excessive debt levels, which can have bearish implications on the dollar.

Budget deficits or surpluses, balance of trade levels and trends also are important fundamentally. This data helps us figure out what the demand is for a country's goods and services, and hence what the demand is for a country's currency. Lastly, inflation levels are important since typically a currency will lose value in inflationary environments since it erodes purchasing power, but then again it may rise because of expectations that central banks will raise rates. This is a good example of why it's difficult to determine how a market will react to specific fundamental information and it illustrates why it's imperative to use technical analysis in conjunction with fundamental analysis.

How do you combine the application of TA and fundamentals in your analysis?

I use fundamentals to determine the major primary driving forces in the markets, and I also use it to determine if the currency is being undervalued or overvalued. I then overlay my shorter-term technical methodology to optimize my pricing for entering and exiting trades.

I also believe that TA is most useful and has the most predictive value in the short to intermediate term. Longer term, fundamental and economic analysis probably has more predictive value

What is the best method of measuring volatility in the FX markets?

Basic statistical studies are always a good start. I have historical data for daily differences in closing prices going back several years and I then use that data to calculate the standard deviation for each currency.

Bollinger Bands are another good way to measure volatility in FX markets. The mean is usually a 20-day simple moving average with two standard deviations above and below the mean defining the bands. If volatility is low, the bands contract and if volatility begins to pick up, the bands expand, which usually signifies the start of a major new trend. I also use the Average True Range (ATR) as a measure of volatility. A range is the difference between the high and low price on any given day, with large ranges indicating high volatility. The ATR is an exponential moving average of the true range.

What determines the 'key levels' in the FX markets?

I use previous long-term pivot levels (support and resistance) and I combine that with major Fibonacci retracement levels to determine key levels in the FX markets (Figure 3). I also use longer-term trend lines, trend channels, and Gann lines.

To what extent are FX markets seasonal? Can you give some examples of seasonality in the currency markets?

Not all FX markets are seasonal in my opinion, but when I've run historical studies of price behavior for various currency pairs I've found that there are several that display seasonality tendencies.

For example, the USD shows strong seasonality against the Euro in the month of January. Many companies and funds repatriate their money back to their local country at the end of the year to dress up their balance sheets and then at the beginning of the year money once again flows abroad for new investment purposes, which could explain this phenomenon.

Is the carry trade still applicable for some currency pairs?

Yes, absolutely, and this has been evident over the past few years. Investors continue to exploit the interest rate differential between currencies which has become an important driver of foreign exchange movements. Prior to the 2007-2009 financial crisis, the yen served as the main carry trade currency, but more recently the US dollar has become the currency of choice to borrow from in order to be able to invest in assets in higher yielding currencies and markets. Also, the yen-funded carry trades for Australia and New Zealand are still very attractive.

In my opinion, carry trades are playing an increasingly larger role in exchange rate movements and it could be the reason we are seeing broader swings in currencies during crises. The carry to risk ratios, a measure of the appeal of carry trades, have been steadily rising over the past decade.

How is the impact on FX rates of the carry trade best measured?

It's difficult to measure the impact that the carry trade has on FX rates and it's difficult to separate speculative investment from investment based on fundamental growth possibilities for example. However, there is little doubt that the carry trade is stoking certain market euphoria in some places exacerbating markets tendencies to already overshoot expectations.

Is it possible to differentiate between times when the market is being driven by speculators and by hedgers?

I don't think it's possible. Nevertheless, I do use the Commitment of Traders (COT) report that is released each week to get a general sense of the amount of commercial traders (hedgers) and non-commercial traders (speculators) and to see the net change from the week before. However, the distinction between commercial and non-commercial traders may be imperfect because the grouping of these traders is based on self identification. Furthermore, because position limits are placed on non-commercial investors, there may be some incentive for traders to self classify as commercial. Also, keep in mind that traders in the futures markets only have to report their positions if they hold a number of contracts above the reporting level defined by the CFTC.

Also, one must take into consideration that the majority of commercial currency trading is done in the spot currency market, so you don't get an accurate representation of real market positioning from the commercial futures positions.

How can intermarket analysis and cross asset correlations be used effectively when analyzing currencies?

Intermarket analysis represents an important component of my analysis given that currencies don't move in isolation – they are part of the global economy and other markets do have an impact on them. Knowing that currencies get affected in various ways from a rise in risk aversion and knowing what signs to look for can help you trade the FX markets. As an example, the dollar and the yen tend to strengthen when there is a flight to safety.

Another example of using intermarket analysis is when studying the so called commodity currencies such as the Canadian dollar or the Australian dollar which are influenced by commodity prices. There is a positive correlation between the price of gold and copper and the Aussie Dollar, and between oil and the Canadian Dollar. It's critical to constantly update cross asset correlations to ensure that the correlations are still valid. For instance, a traditional inverse correlation is for the dollar to trade in the opposite direction of commodity prices, but lately that correlation has broken down.

What is the best source of volume data for the FX markets?

Given that the currency market is decentralized, it's difficult to quantify volume traded at each price level, and so I have to rely on the

17

Commitments of Traders (COT) report to get details on positioning on the futures market. I look for 'extreme positioning' in the currency futures market, which has historically been accurate in identifying trend exhaustion points, and hence important market reversals. I also use open interest (which I view as a secondary trading tool) to gauge the overall health of a specific futures market. Rising and falling open interest levels help to measure the strength or weakness of a particular price trend. For example, if the market has been in a long lasting uptrend with increasing levels of open interest, a leveling off or decrease in open interest is a cautionary sign that the trend may be nearing its end.

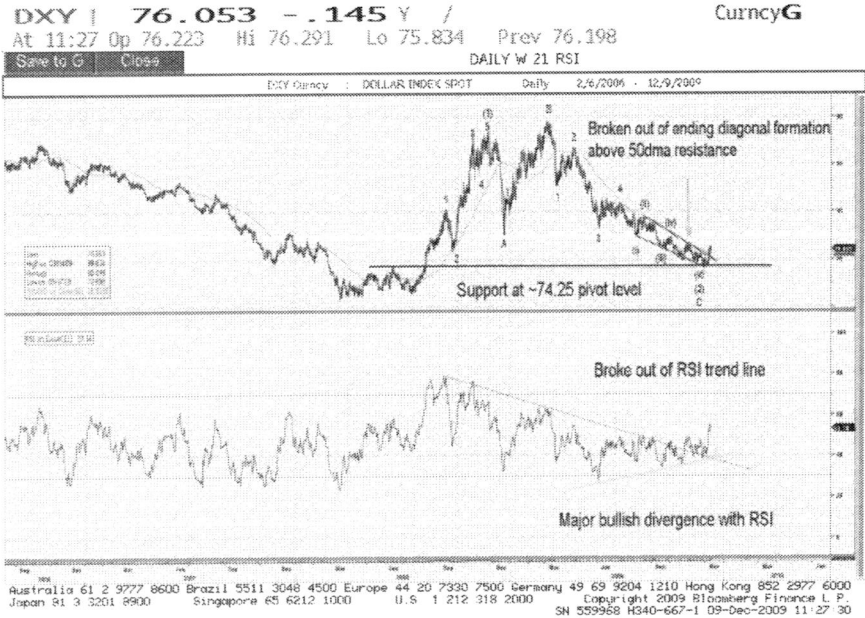

Figure 1: Bullish divergence between price and the RSI

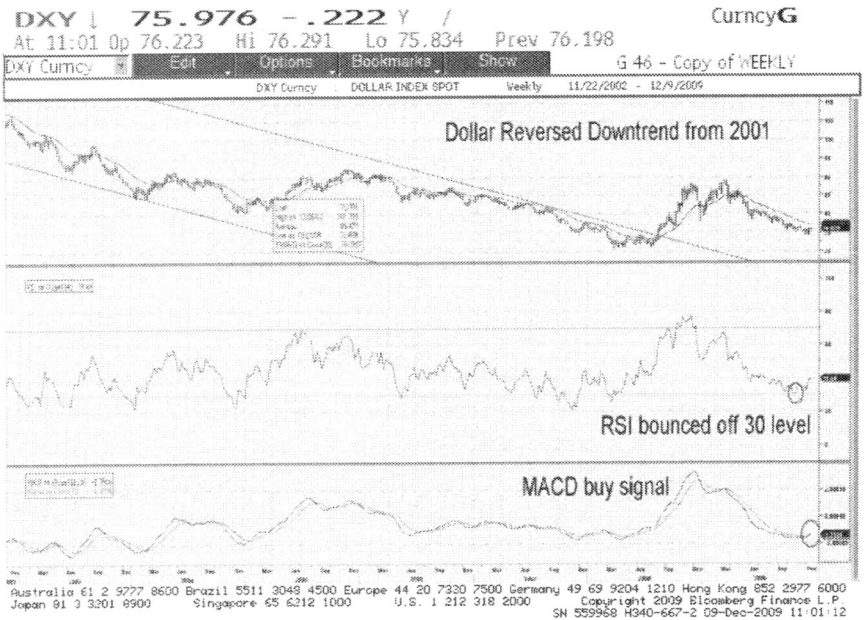

Figure 2: Using the MACD to generate trading signals

Figure 3: Using Fibonacci to determine key levels in EURUSD

Figure 4: Capturing the 5th leg in Elliott Wave for EURUSD

Chapter 2

GEORGE DAVIS

CHIEF TECHNICAL ANALYST

RBC CAPITAL MARKETS

At RBC in Toronto, George Davis specializes in technical analysis of the FX, interest rate and commodity markets with a particular focus on the Canadian dollar. Previously he worded as senior dealer on the spot and forward foreign exchange desks at RBC. George was voted 'Technical Analyst of the Year' at the Technical Analyst magazine's 2010 Awards.

USING TA FOR RESEARCH AND TRADING

Can you explain your basic research style?

My approach to research involves the intermarket application of technical analysis to the various asset classes that I cover. I will often begin my initial analysis by looking for intermarket price patterns, valuation extremes, and price breakouts that confirm one another. If this requirement is fulfilled, it generally tends to strengthen the technical thesis or trade idea that I am putting forth. From there, I will drill down to individual financial instruments, employing candlestick charts, Ichimoku Cloud charts, pattern recognition and indicator valuation analysis as the key components of my approach.

I deal with the whole spectrum of client segments, from commercial to corporate to institutional clients, and they tend to have varying degrees of sophistication and understanding when it comes to technical analysis. Therefore, I try to simplify my research content as much as I can in order to provide value-added insight to the greatest number of clients possible. Pattern and trendline breakouts serve as key inputs that help to determine my views on the markets in this regard, as they tend to visually reinforce my key conclusions.

Which markets do you cover?

I am responsible for technical research involving global foreign exchange, fixed income and commodity markets. Within the FX asset class, the G10 currencies, EUR and CAD crosses, and selected emerging market currencies comprise my coverage universe. In the fixed income world, my focus centers around the US, Canadian, UK, Euro, Australian and New Zealand bond markets, including outright yield analysis, futures markets, curve and inter-market spreads and swap spreads. Our approach to commodities is more targeted, featuring coverage of gold, silver, crude oil, natural gas and base metals. All of these instruments, combined with key global equity indices, form the underlying structure for my intermarket approach.

How does your application of TA differ for short, medium and long-term time scales?

Most of my time is spent on the short and medium-term time scales, with the long-term charts used for primary trend direction and intensity. However, I tend to use the same types of charts, pattern recognition techniques, and indicators regardless of whether I am looking at an hourly, daily, weekly or monthly chart. The key difference is that I will change or modify the settings or parameters for my indicators according to the time period under consideration. All other inputs remain largely the same, with an advantage being more transparent analysis across each time scale.

Do you think that the FX markets are more technically driven than other markets?

I would say that FX markets have definitely become more technically oriented over the years, especially due to the increased participation of hedge funds and model funds. I am most comfortable applying the technical approach to FX markets, followed by fixed income and equity markets. I am least comfortable with commodities as there are often many extraneous variables outside of the markets (weather for example) that can complicate my analysis. These variables often cloud the accuracy of my calls.

Within the FX asset class itself, I find that USD/JPY and the JPY crosses fit the technical approach the best, mainly due to the very strong influence that technical analysis has with Asian market participants. The bottom line is that I do not think that FX markets are necessarily more technically driven than other market segments per se, but at the end of the day, people will find different comfort levels in terms of how, when and to which markets they will apply the discipline of technical analysis.

How 'random' or efficient are the FX markets compared to the equity or fixed income markets?

Some recent academic studies have negated the Random Walk Theory as it pertains to US equity markets, indicating that some trend bias may be present. This provides some compelling arguments with regard to the usefulness of technical analysis for stocks. FX markets are also known to trend very well, which amplifies the importance of the long-term charts as they can be used to identify the primary trend. This, in turn, serves as an overlay which trickles down into my intermediate and short-term analysis.

You always want to trade in the direction of the primary trend from a strategic standpoint, with corrections viewed more as tactical plays. I have not seen much research with regard to the efficiency of fixed income markets. Based on the research that I have seen, equity markets appear to be the most non-random relatively speaking, followed by FX and fixed income markets.

To what extent are the FX markets driven by sentiment? Is this possible to quantify?

I believe that FX markets, and all asset classes for that matter, are driven by varying degrees of sentiment. This is mainly due to the fact that the price mechanism in all markets is driven by human beings. The mood and expectations of participants is reflected in the price of a financial instrument and eventually this filters down to emotions such as fear and greed. Hence, extended bull or bear markets, price blowoffs and selling climaxes are largely a function of prevailing sentiment. This is one of the key reasons why the field of behavioural finance is becoming more important; understanding human psychology and sentiment will allow us to better understand how asset prices are determined.

What are the best sentiment indicators to use?

In the FX world, the IMM Commitment of Traders data is always a basic starting point as a widely followed sentiment indicator. However, the major drawback of this data is the lagged nature of the information as it is released each Friday afternoon but based on positions reported as of the prior Tuesday. Net positions could have easily changed from Tuesday through Friday of the reporting period thus sometimes limiting the usefulness of the information. Nonetheless, I will always be aware of IMM positioning, paying particular attention when positions move to historical extremes. While positioning extremes do not always create an immediate market correction, they do provide a gauge as to the potential magnitude of a corrective phase. In other words, the more extreme the positioning, the more significant pending corrections can become. I often look for trendline breaks in price to confirm the positioning data.

In Figure 1, we have the IMM positioning data for USD/JPY. Note that the 2007 rally in USD/JPY began to lose momentum as short JPY positions moved to very extreme levels in June. This was a hint that the potential for a significant price retracement was increasing. The bearish implications of this development were confirmed when USD/JPY subsequently pierced a key long-term support trendline at 116.51 in August of that year. There was approximately a 2-month lag between the extreme positioning and the long-term trend reversal, but once that signal was confirmed, we saw very good follow-through on the trend reversal.

The Tokyo Financial Exchange reports daily changes in retail margin positions for the JPY against a number of global currencies. Many people are now using this as a sentiment indicator for contrary opinion as the data is more timely in nature. The Daily Sentiment Index has become a popular tool for FX market participants as it is gathered daily and therefore is also more timely. It involves the opinions of small retail traders who are more likely to be wrong at market turning points. Also, many large banks segment their customer flow by client type in an attempt to use that data as a real-time measure of market positioning and sentiment.

Are there any market conditions under which TA works better or worse than other times?

One of the basic tenets of technical analysis is that it is a more effective tool in trending markets, so this would be the most important consideration when I am formulating a thesis. Breakouts conforming to a strong, established trend usually lead to more profitable trading opportunities. For example, in Figure 2, bearish breakouts in USD/CAD during the first three quarters of 2009 year were profitable due to the fact that a strong downtrend was in place. However, upside or downside breakouts since October 2009 have been met with limited success as prices have been "trendless", consolidating within a rectangle pattern as the slope of the 40-day moving average flattens out.

Times of uncertainty or elevated volatility can also benefit from the application of technical analysis. For example, during the credit crisis of 2007-2008, it was extremely difficult to value financial instruments from a fundamental perspective. In many cases, the variation in potential expected outcomes was very, very large. However, using technical analysis allowed you to identify the support and resistance levels that helped define trend intensity and duration. Overlay pattern and valuation analysis within this context and you were able to formulate price targets and assess sentiment to a more accurate degree. In fact, I would say that the discipline of technical analysis was one of the few areas that were able to benefit from the credit crisis in that I noticed that more and more clients were falling back on key price levels and technical concepts in order to get a better grasp of markets. Hopefully, this will lead to a wider following for the technical approach.

INDICATORS AND STRATEGIES

Are there any indicators that work especially well in the FX markets?

I think that the use of indicators comes down to a certain degree of personal preference, comfort and experience through trial and error. Over the years, I have come to favour the use of the momentum and relative strength indicators, along with the slow stochastic study. The latter is my preferred indicator as it is very effective in terms of identifying overbought or oversold conditions as well as bullish or bearish divergences with price. The smoothed nature of the study also tends to provide more accurate buy and sell signals that help to overcome whipsaws.

As an example, Figure 3 features a candlestick chart of USD/CHF with the slow stochastic plotted below the price action. Note that from September to November 2009, three consecutive bullish divergences formed from oversold levels. This preceded the bullish intermediate trend reversal that later took place above 1.0126 in December.

Which settings do you use for momentum and RSI and why?

The momentum and RSI studies are very effective in determining the pace and magnitude of price changes. In terms of the selection of settings for these indicators, the same considerations that apply to moving averages would apply here. That is, one must remember that the shorter the time period chosen as the setting for the indicator, the more sensitive it will be to price moves. As such, shorter time periods are generally associated with not only more trading signals, but also more potentially erroneous signals. Therefore, when I look to select a time period for these indicators I am seeking to derive some sort of balance between the number of signals produced and the accuracy of these signals. As with moving averages, I tend to select settings that are a function of the time period under consideration and the cyclical components of the calendar. For example, on a daily chart, I have found that a 10-day setting for the Momentum or RSI study is useful as it breaks the month up into two half-cycles while balancing the accuracy of the short to medium-term trading signals that are generated. On a weekly chart, I will usually adjust the study settings to 12, effectively splitting the year into quarterly cycles. For monthly charts, I usually use a setting of 12 as well, which generates yearly cycle measurements. I use these studies to not only generate buy and sell signals in the context of trend intensity, but to also help identify overbought or oversold valuation extremes as well as bullish or bearish divergences.

What is your reaction when the charts show a very obvious technical pattern such as a head-and-shoulders or a double top?

Some patterns, such as head-and-shoulders tops or bottoms and double/triple tops tend to be more reliable than others. So, I will always try to assess a pattern in that context. Part of that exercise involves the time duration under consideration; an obvious pattern that forms on a daily chart will carry more weight than one that forms on an hourly chart. The same goes for patterns that form on weekly or monthly charts versus daily charts. I will always take that into consideration. The next step involves identifying the breakout point that will confirm the pattern, as well as the measured move objective of the pattern. That allows for the formulation of a trading strategy where you can begin to assess risk/reward ratios. Pattern analysis, when applied properly, is one of the greatest forecasting benefits that can be derived from the use of technical analysis.

Figure 4 applies this methodology to EUR/JPY. Note that a potential triple top forms against 138.49 between June and October 2009. The bearish implications of this pattern were confirmed in January 2010 when the intervening low at 126.93 was pierced on a daily closing basis. The measured move objective for this pattern is located at 115.37 through June 2010. Note that the slow stochastic study had also issued a sell signal from overbought levels during this time, thus adding momentum to the bearish pattern breakout.

How do you identify when a trend has commenced and may be nearing its end?

My basic starting point for assessing trend commencement or termination always involves the penetration of a key support (in an uptrend) or resistance (in a downtrend) trendline. This may be a very simple approach, but I have found it to be extremely effective. I will often overlay pattern and valuation analysis as part of this process, as these factors often determine the explosiveness of a breakout or reversal and serve to increase accuracy.

For example, in Figure 5, note that GBP/USD posted a bearish long-term trend reversal below the weekly ascending channel base at 2.0239 in December 2007. This channel had been in place for the previous twenty months. Shooting star and evening star patterns had also formed right against the cyclical high at 2.1161 in November 2007. To top things off the weekly slow stochastic study issued a sell signal from overbought levels and a number of long-term bearish divergences were in place (the study was not confirming the move to new highs in price). All of these factors combined to create a bearish backdrop for GBP/USD.

What is the best method for measuring price momentum in the market?

I usually apply the momentum or RSI indicator to measure price momentum. They are great for not only assessing the momentum behind an underlying trend, but they can also be used to pinpoint valuation extremes as well as divergences with price. I also refer to the ADX indicator in order to assess price momentum in the context of whether or not markets are in a trending mode. The Rate of Change

(ROC) study is another tool that can be used to gauge price momentum or intensity.

Figure 6 is an example of the application of the ROC study. Note the transition from positive to negative price momentum in October-November 2009 after the formation of a double top pattern. This was followed by a bearish trend reversal for both GBP/CAD and the ROC. Another period of negative price momentum was in place in February 2010.

Do you use Fibonacci, Gann or Elliott Wave techniques and if so, how?

The first thing that I will do whenever I see a trend reversal of any time frame is to apply Fibonacci ratios to the prior trend. This is beneficial in two ways: (1) it helps to establish potential price targets for the trend reversal at hand and (2) it helps to assess whether the reversal will just be part of a corrective phase or an actual full-blown trend change. Fibonacci retracement levels are also helpful in identifying support and resistance levels as part of longer-term trend progressions.

I have a difficult time applying Elliott Wave analysis to short-term charts and sometimes even medium-term applications find me frequently using alternate wave counts that serve to reduce the accuracy of my calls. However, I am very comfortable in using Elliott Wave counts on long-term charts as I find that the price cycles are easier to identify. This allows me to assess price moves in the context of trend continuation or retracement scenarios. Also, many of the Elliott Wave principles involve the application of Fibonacci price and time projections, so these two methodologies often work well together. I do not utilize Gann analysis in my work.

Figure 7 provides an example of how I apply Fibonacci and Elliott Wave analysis in the FX markets. Note that USD/CAD forms a bullish engulfing month and key reversal month in November 2007 that completes the 5th impulsive wave of an Elliott Wave structure. The monthly studies were also tracing out a bullish divergence from oversold levels. This was followed by a bullish long-term trend reversal above 1.0485 in August 2008 as an A-B-C correction was underway. In terms of potential topside retracement targets, the 23.6% retracement level at 1.1007 was quickly attained, shifting the focus up to the 38.2% Fibonacci retracement level at 1.1995, followed by 50% retracement at 1.2794 and 61.8% retracement at 1.3592.

28

Notice how the 50% retracement level was tested for seven consecutive months – but prices failed to register a monthly close above this key level as the monthly studies eventually issued a sell signal from overbought levels. In effect, this indicated that the A-B-C corrective phase was coming to an end and was followed by a resumption of the downtrend as USD/CAD pushed back toward parity.

How do you use moving averages? If so, which periodicities do you use and do you use them directly to generate trade signals?

Like many, I tend to use moving averages as an assessment of trend over various time horizons. I view them as "curvilinear trendlines" so to speak. I usually use 5 and 10-day moving averages to assess short-term trend dynamics, 20 and 40-day moving averages for medium-term trend assessment, and 100 and 200-day moving averages for longer-term trend analysis. The periodicities that I use are often related to calendar cycles (1-week, 2-week, 1-month, 2-month, 1-year, etc). I will often use 20 and 40-day crossovers for medium-term trade signals and 40 and 200-day crossovers for longer-term signals.

Unlike others, I use the 40 and 200-day crossover to generate the so-called "Golden" or "Death Cross" as opposed to the 50 and 200-day crossover that is commonly used. Again, these numbers fit my time cycles more optimally. I also pay attention to the slope of the moving averages during crossovers. For example, if a Golden Cross takes place while both moving averages are increasing in value, I would generally consider this as a stronger bullish signal because the slope of the moving averages is conforming to both the signal and underlying trend.

In Figure 8, EUR/USD commenced a bearish trend in December 2009 that was amplified by the pair breaking below the 40-day moving average. As the downtrend progressed, the 40-day moving average pierced the 200-day moving average from above in February 2010, thereby producing the so-called "Death Cross". The slope of the 200-day moving average subsequently levelled out and has begun to move into negative territory, adding some weight to the Death Cross.

If prices reach a major support level do you wait until it has broken through before buying or selling?

I would classify my approach to breakouts as conservative in nature as I do not trade an inter-period break of a price level. Rather, I like to employ the close for the period in question as a filter in order to avoid whipsaws or false-breaks. Hence, on an hourly chart, I would use an hourly close below the support in order to confirm a bearish breakout. Similarly, I would employ a daily close on the daily chart, a weekly close on the weekly chart and a monthly close on the monthly chart in order to confirm breakouts.

For example, Figure 9 illustrates the application of a closing filter on NZD/USD. Note that prices broke above resistance at 0.7018 on an intraday basis on February 23, 2010 but failed to close above this key level. Those who went long on the intraday break would have had to suffer through a subsequent pullback to 0.6843 two days later and may have even been stopped out. Those who employed the daily close as a filter would have had no position and thus avoided a potential drawdown. Moreover, employing such a filter would have enabled the execution of a long position in NZD/USD at a more advantageous rate of 0.6971 on February 26, 2010 – when prices actually registered a daily close above the trendline in order to confirm a bullish trend reversal.

How do you judge if a market is overbought or oversold?

I tend to rely on the slow stochastic indicator in order to determine whether or not a market is overbought or oversold. However, I use a more restrictive filter in the sense that I employ 20% as my oversold threshold and 80% as overbought – as opposed to the more conventional measures of 25% and 75% respectively.

Although this might generate fewer signals, the signals tend to be slightly more accurate by using a stricter valuation trigger. I often overlay this with the RSI, using 20% and 80% as my trigger points as well. If I see either of these indicators at an extreme, I will also fall back on the IMM positioning data in order to assess whether or not FX sentiment appears to be at an extreme.

Figure 10 provides an example of using the slow stochastic indicator and RSI to identify overbought price conditions. AUD/USD struggled to sustain moves above the 0.9300 level in January 2010 as both the slow stochastic and RSI moved into overbought territory above the 80% threshold on both metrics. Note that this was also accompanied by the formation of bearish divergences, which increased the probability of a potential trend reversal developing. This was confirmed on January 26, 2010, when prices registered a daily close below the key support trendline at 0.9022.

CHARACTERISTICS UNIQUE TO THE FX MARKETS

What intraday effects impact the FX markets?

The various country economic data releases can obviously have an impact on markets if they deviate substantially from consensus expectations. Ad hoc statements from government or central bank officials can also have a short-term market impact, as can unexpected events such as a terrorist attack or a ratings action from one of the major rating agencies such as Moodys, Standard & Poors or Fitch.

The various fixings that take place globally throughout the trading day are generating more and more volatility because many fund and portfolio managers are now benchmarking themselves to the fixing value. Large barrier options and option strikes can also have an intraday impact on FX markets. Last but not least, depending on the depth and liquidity of the currency pair in question, large order flows or clusters of stop loss orders can also cause short-term price distortions.

How far out do you analyse the FX markets? What specific strategies do you use for longer-term analysis?

My analysis tends to extend out to two years in terms of time horizon. However, beyond the one-year horizon, I have found that forecasting accuracy tends to trail off significantly. As a result, most client queries tend to focus on the six to 12-month time frame. In terms of strategies, I tend to utilize major trendline breakouts in conjunction with Elliott Wave analysis and Fibonacci retracement ratios as the key inputs to derive price targets as well as assess risk/reward ratios.

In Figure 11, EUR/USD posted a bearish long-term trend reversal below 1.4014 in October 2008. This was the first hint that a major shift in sentiment was underway that had significant implications for long-term forecasts. The fact that an impulsive Elliott Wave structure was in place with the formation of a double top only added to the bearish potential that was present – as did the bearish study divergence that had formed from overbought levels. This exposed

31

38.2% Fibonacci retracement at 1.3058 as one potential downside target, followed by 50% Fibonacci retracement at 1.2137 and 61.8% retracement at 1.1217. Notice how the 50% retracement level has contained the decline so far, allowing for the establishment of a redrawn trendline at 1.2963 that now serves as a key support level to watch going forward.

Is there any difference in your approach between the analysis of G7 and emerging markets currencies? To what extent is liquidity in emerging markets a factor?

I generally try to apply a standardized approach when analyzing the G7 and emerging markets, using candlestick charts and the slow stochastic study again as key inputs for both segments. However, liquidity is definitely a primary concern for the EM segment as the lack of depth can often cause false breakouts or erroneous pattern breakouts. Some currency pairs, such as USD/MXN and USD/BRL, have seen improvements in liquidity and accompanying signals over time, but many other pairs still suffer from liquidity concerns. Sometimes I will consider implementing a stricter two-day closing rule to EM market breakouts in order to limit and minimize whipsaws as much as possible (as opposed to the standard one-day closing rule that I generally use).

Figure 12 provides an example of the application of a stricter two-day closing rule to USD/BRL and the potential benefits derived from a tougher price filter. Notice that the implementation of this rule prevented a false break below 1.8346 on February 2, 2010. Prices subsequently rallied to a high of 1.8929 before moving lower again. Hence, the stricter filter rule would have prevented a potential drawdown from taking place. Note that the February 17, 2010 close below 1.8598 not only confirmed a bearish trend reversal – it was also followed by a deeper selloff to a low of 1.7915. Such filers are not perfect as the extra day of waiting for confirmation can lead to a less advantageous entry level, but they can sometimes prevent premature entry into a trade, as this example demonstrates.

To what extent do you look at fundamental information?

I follow all of the major fundamental data releases in order to assess the economic backdrop and keep abreast of developments. I will often examine the price action relative to the data releases in order to assess market sentiment, positioning and expectations. If the price reaction does not reflect what would be expected from the data outcome, I will go back and check my charts to see if any important breakouts are taking place. At the end of the day though, I will always resort to the analysis of pure price action in order to determine my view on the market in question. This is mainly due to the fact that the price mechanism is forward-looking in nature. Hence, the charts will often show key turning points in markets ahead of the fundamental data. In my opinion, this is one of the key advantages of using the technical approach.

What fundamental information is most important for the FX markets?
The fundamental themes that impact the market tend to shift over time. I remember when I first began in the markets in the early 1990's, the US money supply data would often move the markets as much as the non-farm payrolls report. A few years ago, the Treasury International Capital System (TICS) data was watched closely in order to assess if there were sufficient inflows to finance the bulging US deficit. In the current environment, employment, retail sales, consumer confidence and housing data is key in terms of assessing the sustainability of the economic recovery. I think that as we progress into 2011 and 2012, the inflation data may become more of a focal point for the market as interest rate expectations begin to shift and get re-priced.

What is the best method of measuring volatility in the FX markets?
I do not spend a great deal of my time assessing FX market volatility. However, I do watch implied and historical volatility levels for options on the major currency pairs. More people are also paying attention to the ECB's Global Hazard Index with regard to FX volatility, as this metric assesses implied volatility via options on EUR/USD, USD/JPY and EUR/JPY. From a technical perspective, the Average True Range (ATR) as well as Bollinger Bands can be used to gauge volatility levels, so I will look at those indicators from time to time, especially if a breakout is at hand or underway.

Figure 13 demonstrates the overlay of Bollinger Bands on to the EUR/JPY cross as well as the application of the ATR. Notice that the bearish breakdown in January 2010 caused the cross to hug the lower boundary of the Bollinger Bands while the ATR indicator spiked higher. This indicated that elevated levels of volatility accompanied the breakdown in EUR/JPY as prices accelerated lower.

Are the currency markets more or less prone to trending than stocks?

From the academic studies that I have seen, more and more evidence is surfacing that rejects the Random Walk Theory for equity markets. This would suggest that trending characteristics are present in stocks at a more elevated level than FX markets. However, that does not necessarily mean that FX markets do not also trend. The increased participation of model-based hedge funds in the FX markets is indicative that some trending behaviour is present, as many of these fund use algorithms that attempt to identify and profit from unfolding trends.

Figure 14 provides a general example of trending periods in FX markets. Note that the DXY was in a defined uptrend from 1995 until 2002, with the subsequent reversal setting the stage for a bearish trend that was in place from 2002 through 2008. The period from 2008 to the present has been defined by a sideways or trendless market.

Are there any specific currency pairs that are more prone to trending?

I do not necessarily view any specific currency pairs as more prone to trending behaviour than others. However, I would say that USD/JPY and the JPY crosses often tend to trade very well using the technical approach as there is a high concentration of technical practitioners in the Asian markets. Also, due to liquidity considerations, the emerging market currencies tend to have higher levels of volatility and more associated noise, which may provide more of a challenge to identify price trends at times. I will sometimes fall back on the ADX indicator as a barometer to gauge whether or not a currency pair is in trending mode.

What determines the 'key levels' in the FX markets?

A number of factors are at play in the determination of key price levels. Round numbers often serve as a psychological anchor for the market, with stop-loss and barrier option orders clustered around these crucial price points. Support and resistance trendlines also create key price levels that are watched, with the longer that the trendline has been in effect and the more times that it has been tested increasing the importance and significance of the price level. Finally, price patterns such as double and triple tops will expose key price levels to the market where bearish sentiment begins to prevail (and vice-versa for double and triple bottoms of course).

Figure 15 discusses some key price levels for USD/CHF. Note that the parity area provided psychological support to the market between October and December 2009. Prices subsequently generated a bullish intermediate trend reversal above 1.0126 in December that has led to the creation of an ascending channel pattern as the 200-day moving average was exceeded. The channel base at 1.0343 serves as key support now, with the channel top at 1.1000 serving as resistance.

To what extent are FX markets seasonal? Can you give some examples of seasonality in the currency markets?

FX markets do sometimes display seasonal characteristics. For example, calendar year-end repatriation of profits from US corporations can sometimes create seasonal demand for the USD. Funding requirements over the year-end turn can also serve as a factor here. The Japanese year-end in March can also lead to some repatriation flows that have an impact on the JPY. Some people have attempted to identify so-called "January effects" for EUR/USD and USD/JPY. As such, market participants watch these themes and sometimes attempt to exploit them.

How do you measure the impact that fund flows have on specific currencies?

I tend to use the IMM Commitment of Traders data as a gauge of fund participation in any specific currency pair. One method that I find particularly useful is to assess the total outstanding positions of non-commercial accounts as a percentage of total open interest. Using this metric, one can assess the outstanding positions from speculative accounts relative to total open interest. The historical tracking of this metric can be used as a proxy for the impact that hedge funds are having on specific currencies and associated sentiment.

Figure 16 provides an example of measuring the percentage of open interest that is controlled by speculative accounts for EUR/USD. Note that the prior extreme in short positions of 40.6% has recently been exceeded, with the percentage of open interest currently standing at 59.4%. This does not imply that we will see a price reversal right away, but it does cause me to start watching resistance levels that, if triggered, are likely to produce a significant short covering rally.

Is it true that currencies are especially susceptible to markets rumours? If so, why is this?

I think that all markets are susceptible to rumours. Recall that as the credit crisis progressed through 2007 and 2008, there were persistent rumours that made their way through credit and equity markets and they also had in intermarket impact on FX markets via rising and declining levels of risk aversion. Rumours of large deal flows, option strikes and central bank intervention appear at various intervals, with levels of volatility and uncertainty often determining how much of an impact the rumour in question may have. I have found that during periods of heightened volatility and uncertainty, rumours tend to have more of a market impact as market participants are less confident in their views and associated positions. During these times, positions are more apt to be put on or reversed in part due to market rumours.

Is the carry trade still applicable for some currency pairs?

The risk aversion theme is a major factor that is determining directional bias in FX markets at the moment. The carry trade is an offshoot of this theme in the sense that a decrease in levels of risk aversion tend to promote or encourage carry trades as participants are more willing to take on increased levels of risk at the margin. The opposite takes place when risk aversion levels increase as participants shy away from riskier trades.

What has changed over time are the currencies that have been used as vehicles for the carry trade. The JPY was in vogue in this regard from approximately 2003 to 2007 as Japanese interest rates were among the lowest in the world – thus making it more attractive to sell (or borrow) JPY and use the proceeds to invest in higher yielding currencies. The credit crisis changed the dynamic because as the US Federal Reserve slashed US interest rates aggressively in order to provide liquidity to the market, the USD slowly began to replace the JPY as the favoured low-yielding currency to fund the carry trade.

How is the impact on FX rates of the carry trade best measured?

One of the indicators that I have used to gauge the impact of the carry trade is the ratio of the S&P500 Index to JPY, which is contained in Figure 17. The sharp rally in this intermarket relationship from 2004 through mid-2007 was characterized by a decrease in risk aversion and an increase in carry trades and leverage ratios. The completion of a head-and-shoulders pattern in 2008 suggested that the carry trade was coming under pressure and served as a precursor to the great deleveraging process that took place thereafter as the credit crisis grew.

Is it possible to differentiate between times when the market is being driven by speculators and by hedgers?

The increased participation of hedge funds in FX markets has led to a situation whereby hedging flows are often overshadowed by speculative turnover. The main reason for this development is that hedging flows are usually medium to long-term in nature and more infrequent in terms of occurrence. Speculative flows take on the opposite characteristics in that a large portion of the turnover is short to medium-term in nature defined by frequent amounts of transactions. Using the IMM Commitment of Traders data, monitoring levels of risk aversion as well as carry trade metrics makes me more comfortable in assessing when speculative accounts may or may not be driving price action in the markets.

How can intermarket analysis and cross asset correlations be used effectively when analysing currencies?

I have found that intermarket analysis is an extremely useful tool to employ as part of my approach to analyzing and forecasting FX markets. First and foremost, I am much more confident in my view if a price breakout in a currency pair is corroborated by price action in one or more of the other asset classes. This tends to increase the accuracy of my forecast. Secondly, the use of cross asset correlations is often very beneficial as they help to explain some of the key themes that are driving financial markets. In addition, this metric can identify potential shifts in themes – periods when certain variables become less significant and others become more relevant in helping to explain price action. These shifts can be detected as the correlation coefficients increase or decrease in value. Over the years, I have found that I am relying more and more on intermarket analysis in order to develop a top-down view of the various asset classes and the rotation that takes place among them.

Figure 18 provides an example of cross asset correlations and intermarket analysis, using one-year rolling correlations between USD/CAD and (1) world equity markets, (2) crude oil, (3) base metals and (4) 2-year Canada-US swap spreads. Note that there was a significant shift in the cross asset correlations in 2008 as the credit crisis deepened. This caused crude oil to be a much less significant correlation variable, while global equity markets increased dramatically in importance. This reflected the fact that equity markets were being used as a proxy for risk aversion. This remains the case today, although note that the importance of crude oil is starting to increase dramatically again.

Taking these conclusions one step further, Figure 19 plots the intermarket relationship between the Canadian dollar and the S&P500 Index. Note that the CAD pierced a key support level at 0.9556 in January at the same time that the S&P500 pierced support at 1125.21. Hence, the bearish breakdown in the CAD was being confirmed by the breakdown in equities, reinforcing the cross asset relationship.

Finally, Figure 20 takes a look at the intermarket relationship between the CAD and crude oil. Of note, crude oil pierced support at 75.28 in December, followed by the CAD breaking support at 0.9556 in January. Therefore, we have a number of factors that are confirming and validating the bearish breakdown in the CAD. These results would add conviction to my bearish CAD thesis and likely increase the accuracy of the bearish CAD signal that is being generated. The bottom line is that the more factors that appear to substantiate your thesis, the better the chance that it will be validated, thus enhancing the accuracy of your calls.

Do you keep an eye on volume levels and if so, how do you use them in your decisions? What is the best source of volume data for the FX markets?

Unlike stock and futures markets, volume is more difficult to quantify accurately in FX markets. This is largely due to the fact that most stock and futures trading takes place in a centralized marketplace. FX, on the other hand, is mainly an over-the-counter market. With different banks all around the world executing a number of different trades in various currency pairs at any given time, it is difficult to obtain an accurate measure of volume. Sometimes turnover in the IMM currency futures can be used as a proxy for volume, but again, this has significant limitations as most transactions take place in the OTC market.

With the advent of screen-based trading platforms, some market participants are now using the number of trades (each time a bid is hit or an offer is taken) as an approximation for volume. This may be one of the more accurate measures of volume available on a real-time basis.

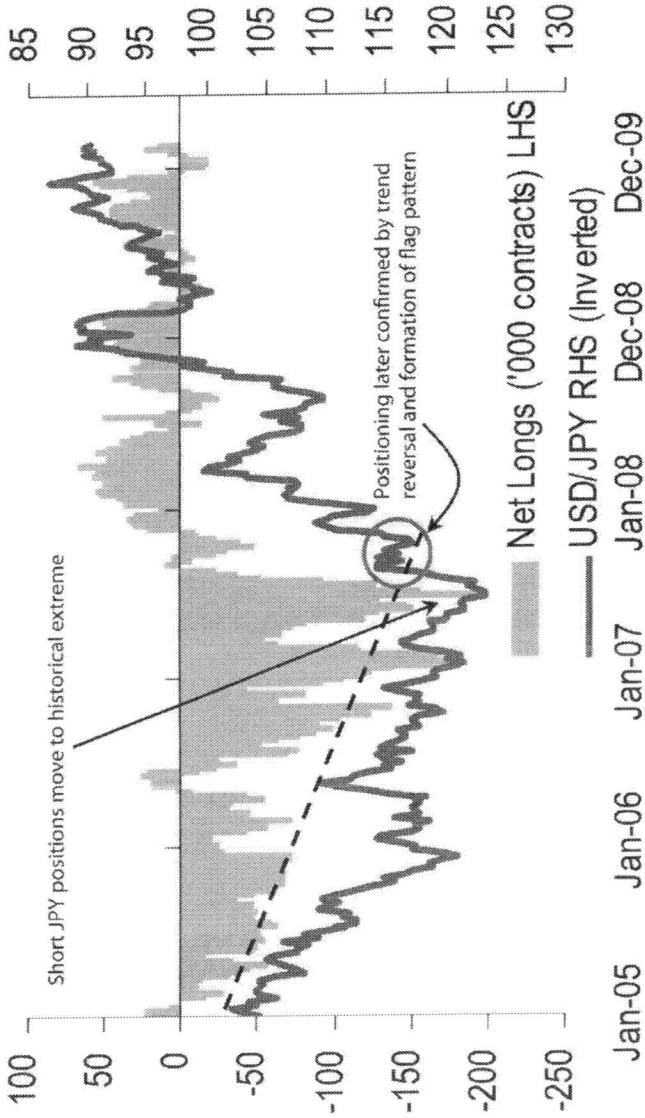

Figure 1: IMM Positioning, Sentiment and Contrary Opinion for USD/JPY

Source: Bloomberg

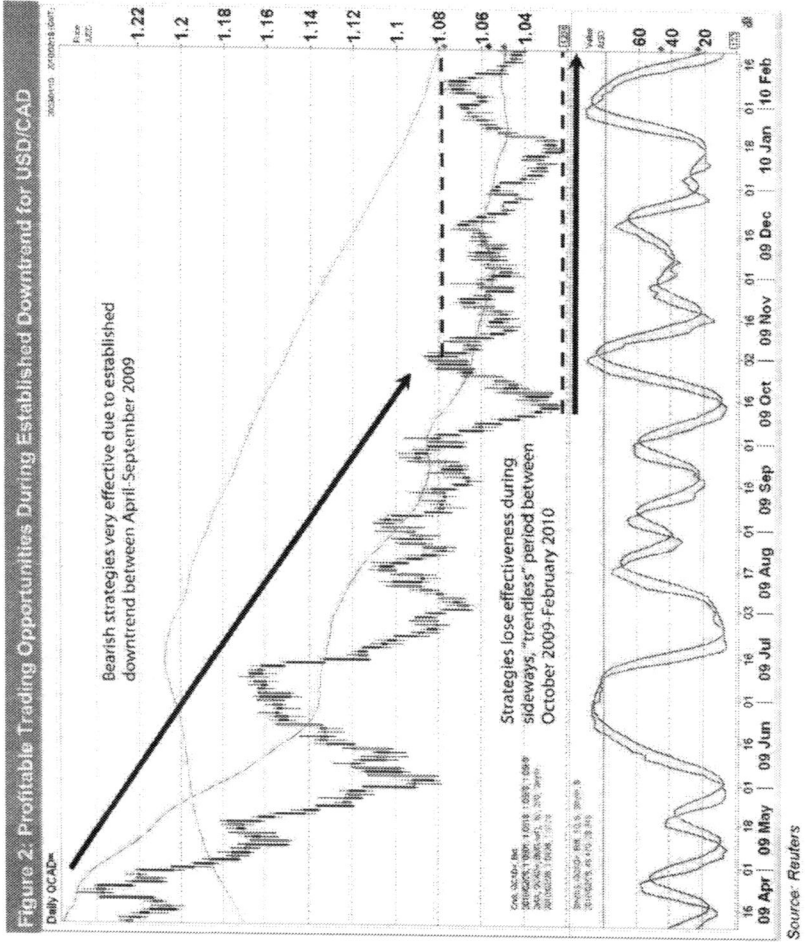

Figure 2: Profitable Trading Opportunities During Established Downtrend for USD/CAD

Bearish strategies very effective due to established downtrend between April-September 2009

Strategies lose effectiveness during sideways, "trendless" period between October 2009-February 2010

Source: *Reuters*

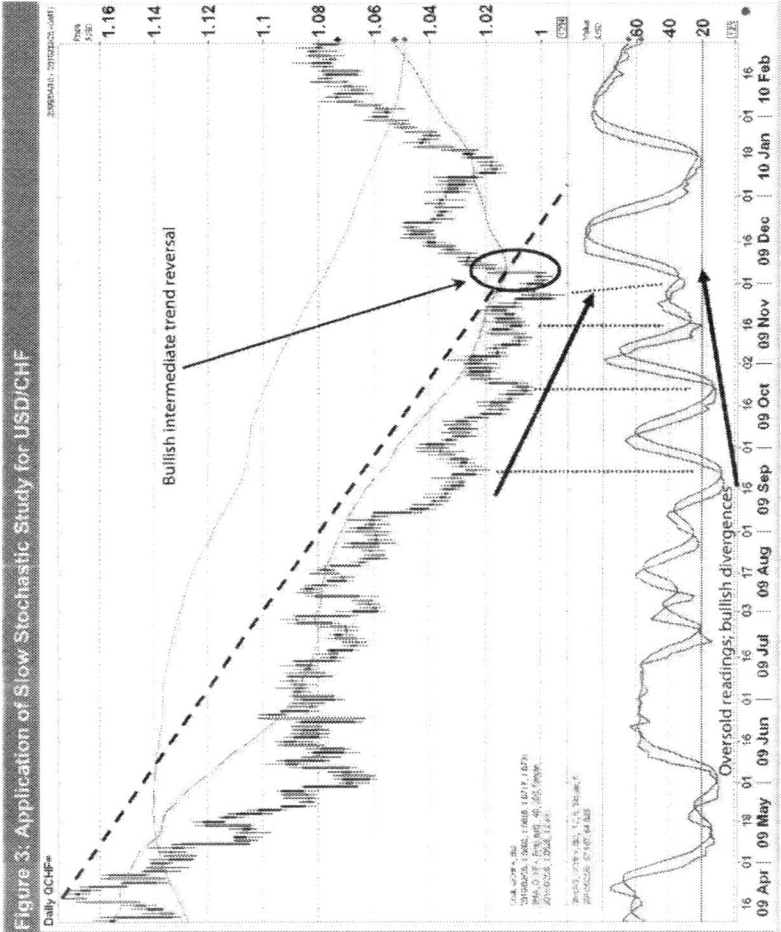

Figure 3: Application of Slow Stochastic Study for USD/CHF

Bullish intermediate trend reversal

Oversold readings; bullish divergences

Daily QCHF=

Source: Reuters

41

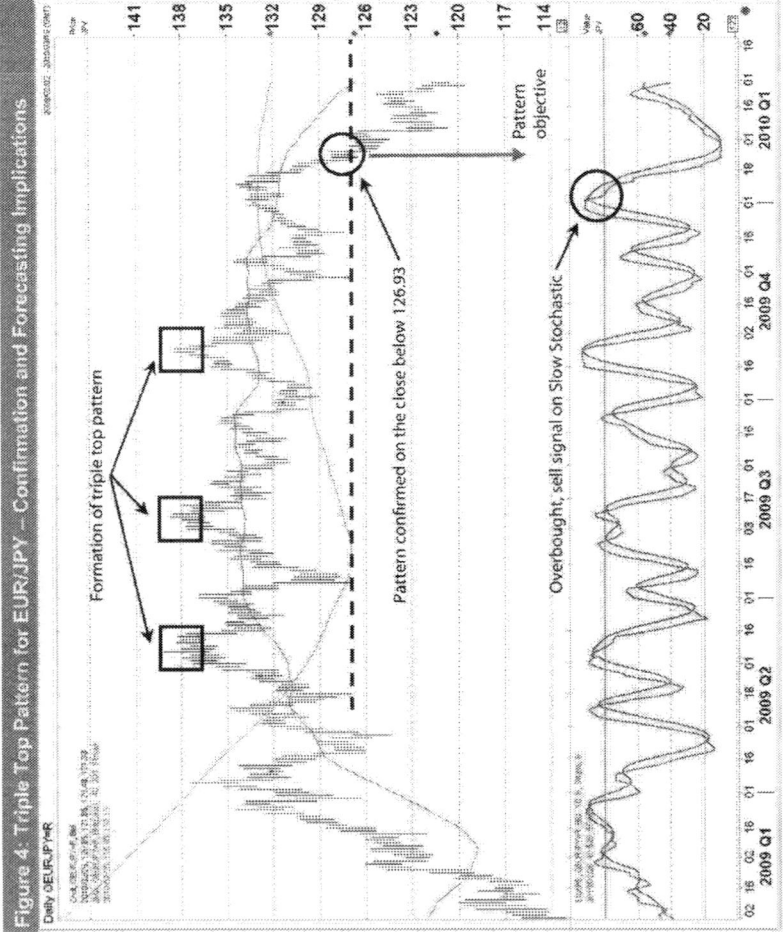

Figure 4: Triple Top Pattern for EUR/JPY – Confirmation and Forecasting Implications

Source: Reuters

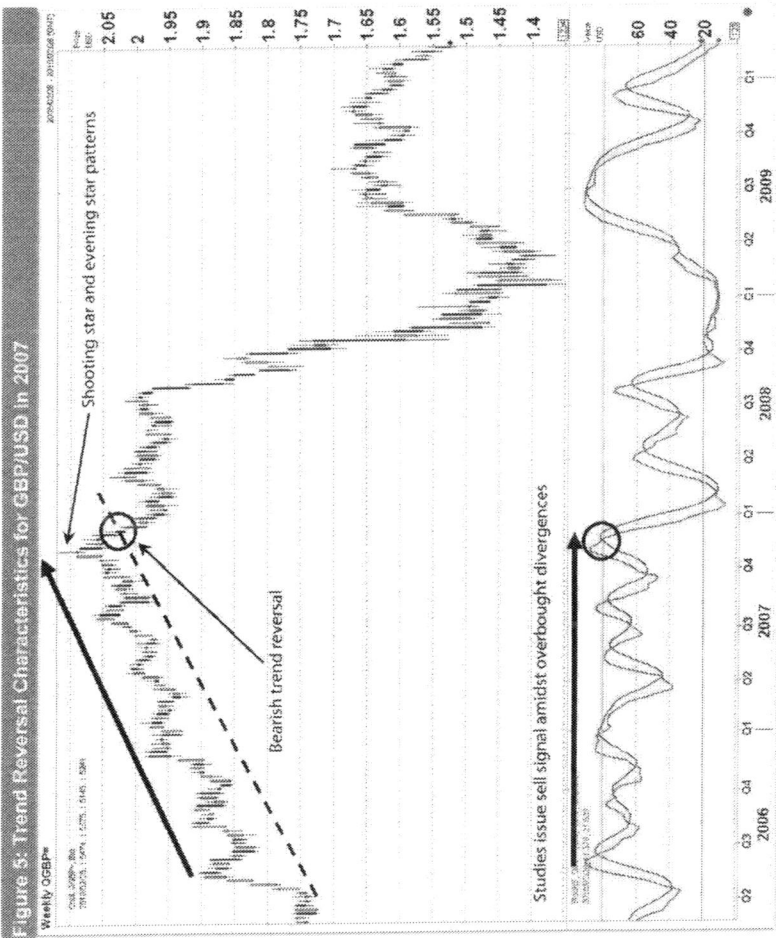

Figure 5: Trend Reversal Characteristics for GBP/USD in 2007

43

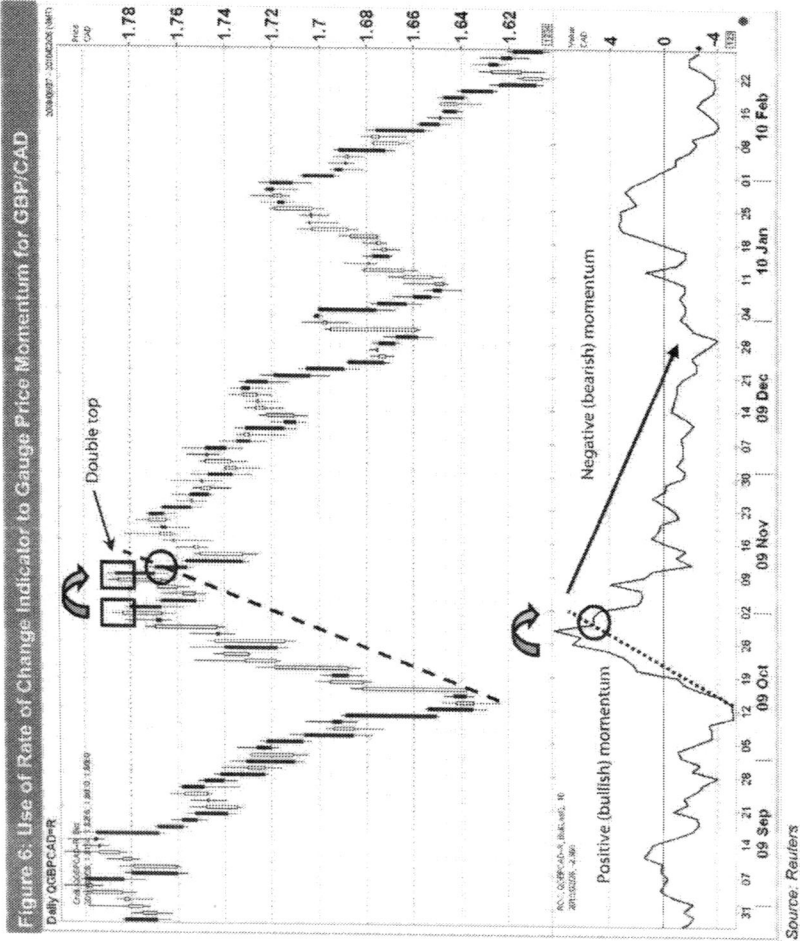

Figure 6: Use of Rate of Change Indicator to Gauge Price Momentum for GBP/CAD

Source: Reuters

Figure 7: Elliott Wave and Fibonacci Retracement Analysis Applied to USD/CAD

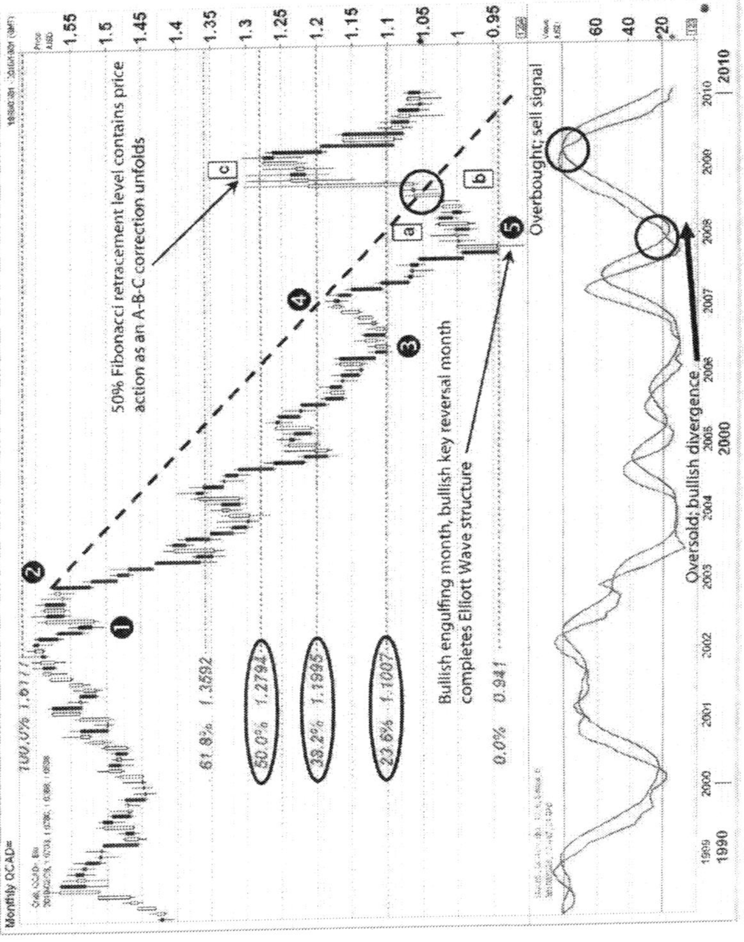

Monthly QCAD=

100.0% 1.6177

50% Fibonacci retracement level contains price action as an A-B-C correction unfolds

c

61.8% 1.3592

50.0% 1.2794

38.2% 1.1995

23.6% 1.1007

0.0% 0.941

a

b

Bullish engulfing month, bullish key reversal month completes Elliott Wave structure

Overbought; sell signal

Oversold; bullish divergence

2000

1990   2000   2001   2002   2003   2004   2005   2006   2007   2008   2010

1989   2010   2010

Price CAD

1.55
1.5
1.45
1.4
1.35
1.3
1.25
1.2
1.15
1.1
1.05
1
0.95

60
40
20

Source: Reuters

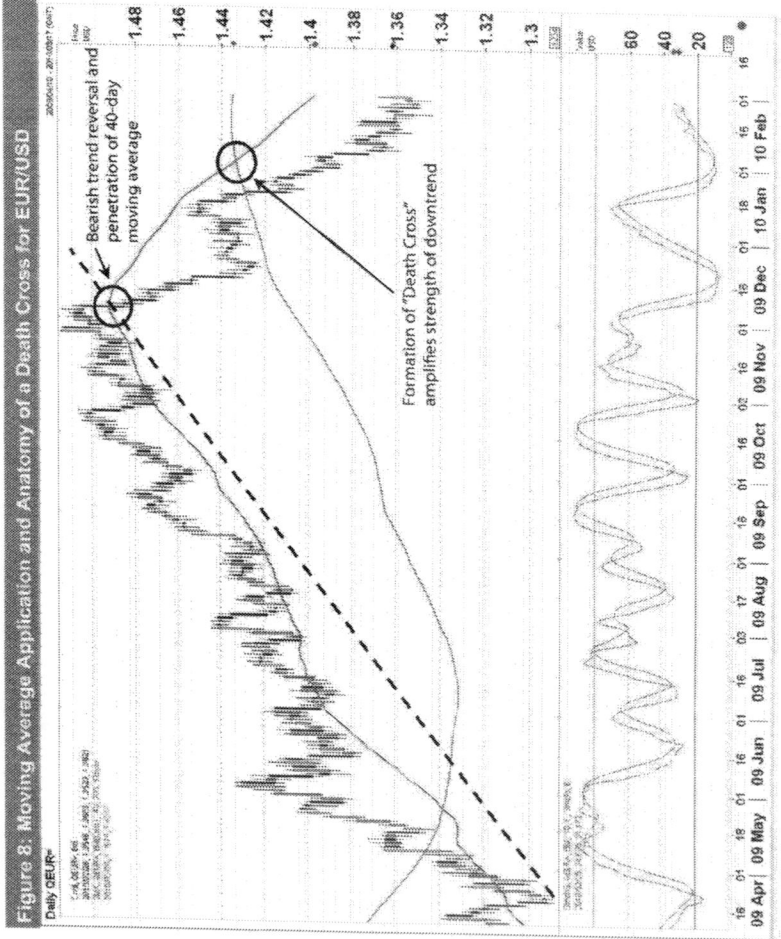

Figure 8: Moving Average Application and Anatomy of a Death Cross for EUR/USD

Bearish trend reversal and penetration of 40-day moving average

Formation of "Death Cross" amplifies strength of downtrend

Source: Reuters

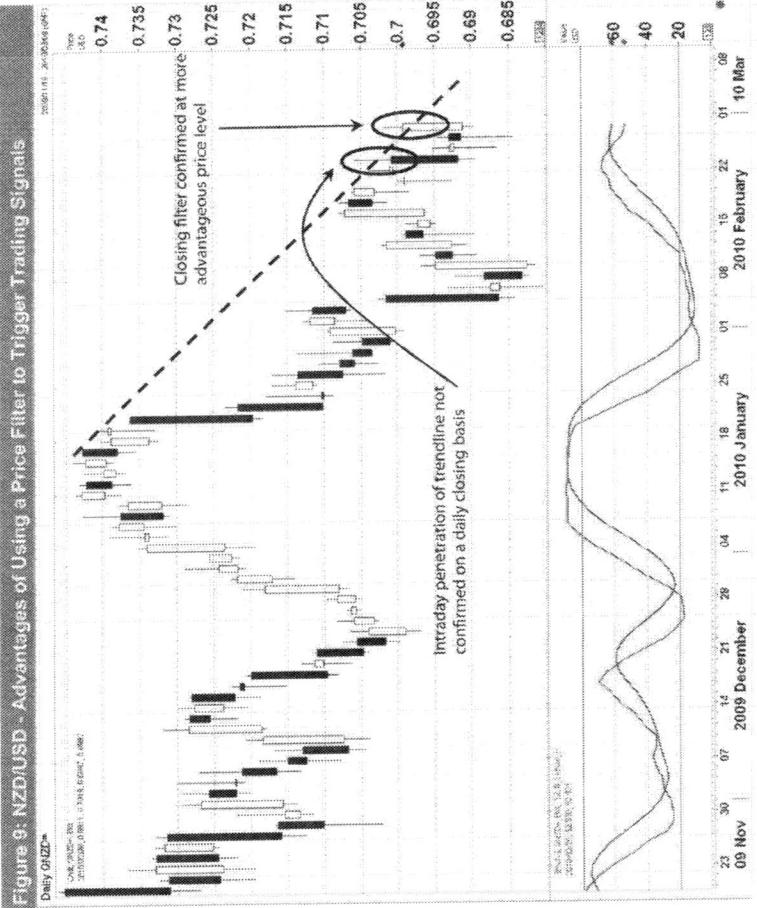

Figure 9: NZD/USD - Advantages of Using a Price Filter to Trigger Trading Signals

Source: Reuters

47

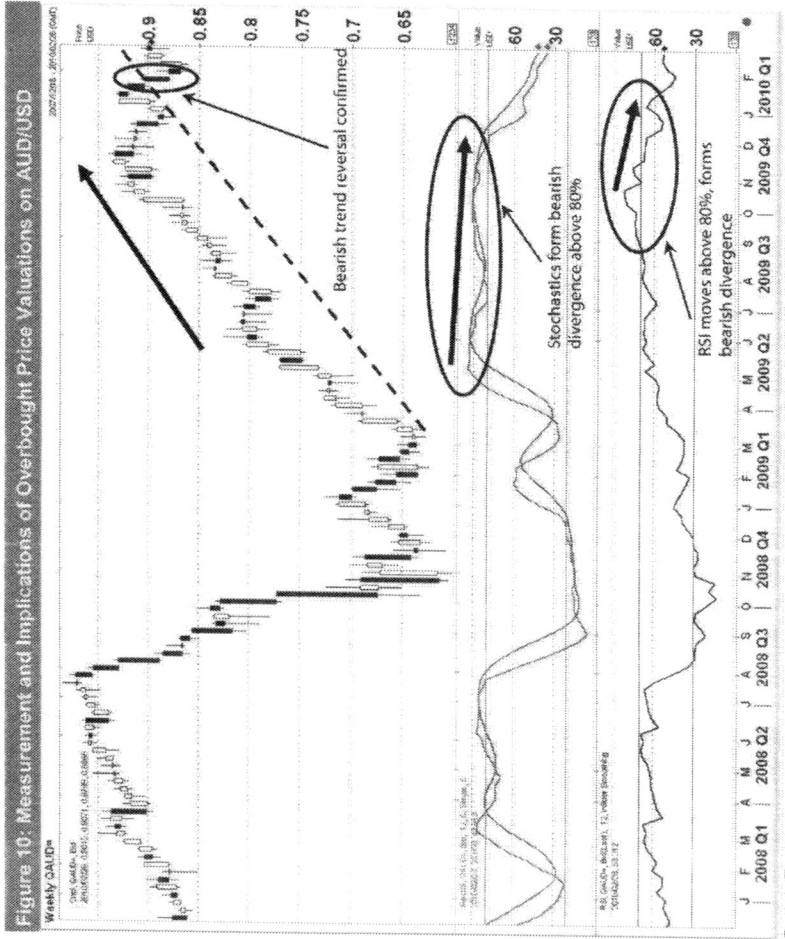

Figure 10: Measurement and Implications of Overbought Price Valuations on AUD/USD

Source: Reuters

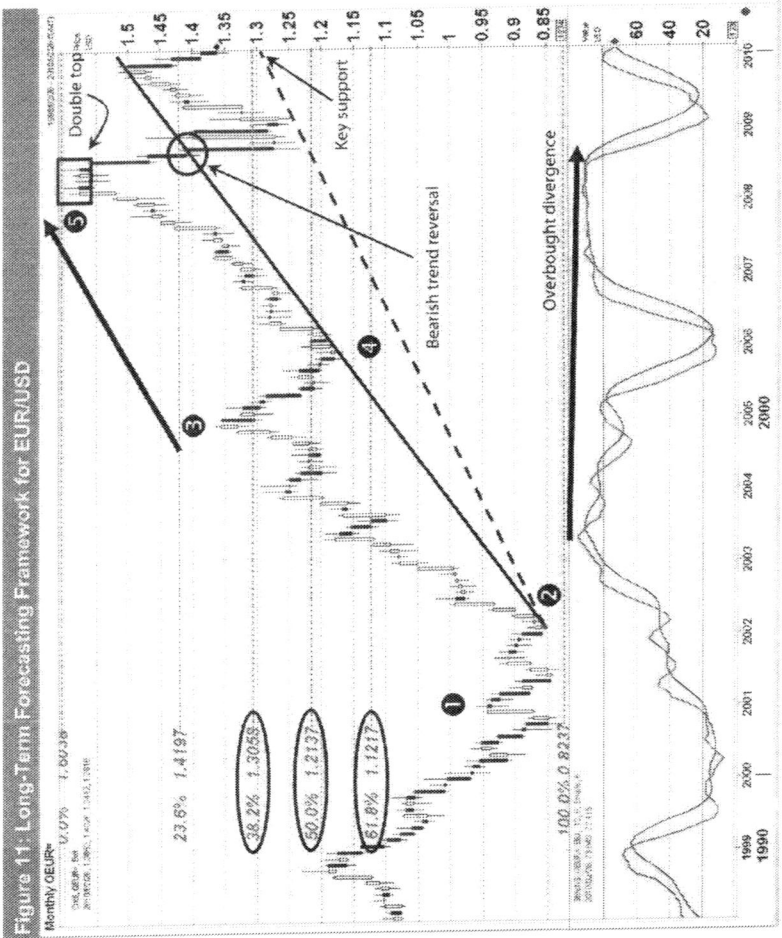

Figure 11: Long-Term Forecasting Framework for EUR/USD

Source: Reuters

49

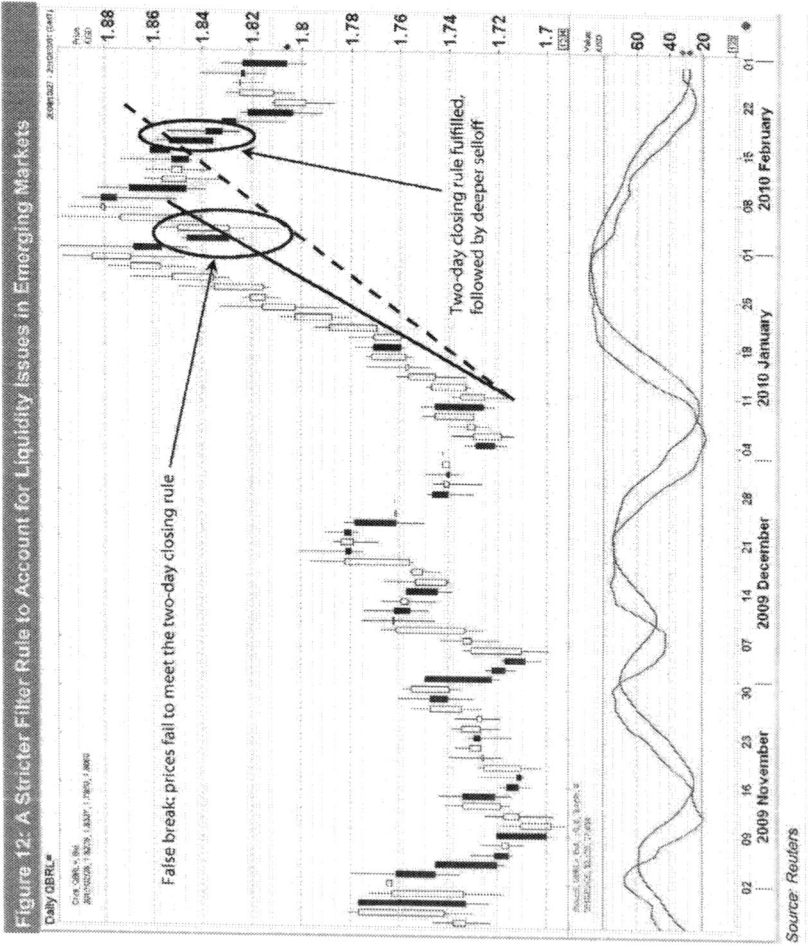

Figure 12: A Stricter Filter Rule to Account for Liquidity Issues in Emerging Markets

Source: Reuters

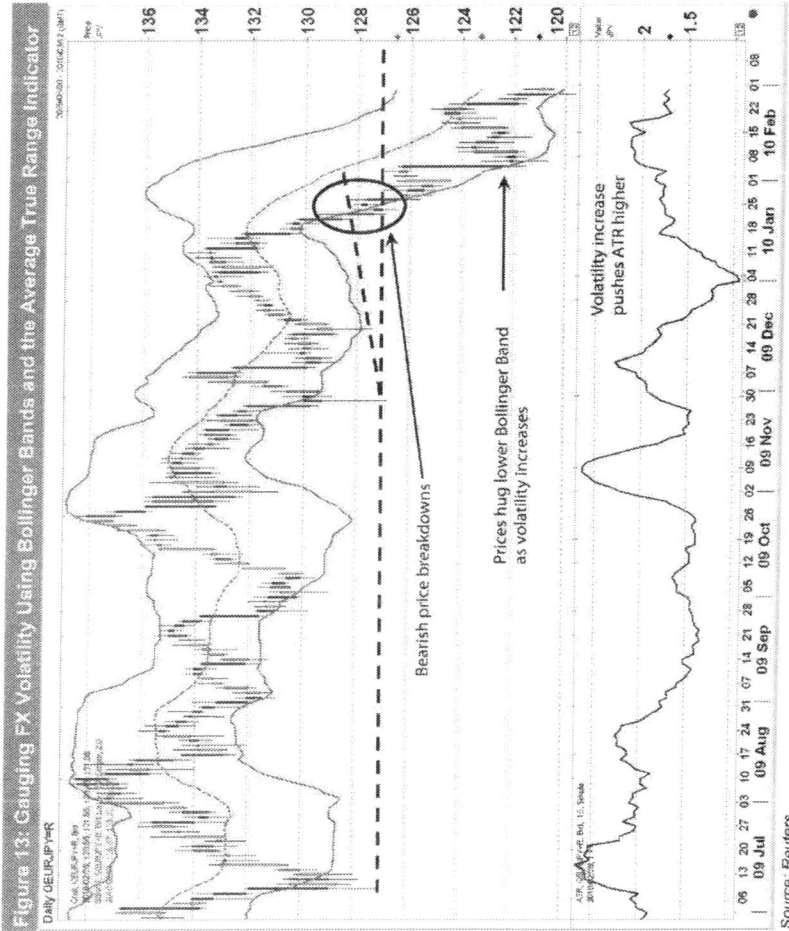

Figure 13: Gauging FX Volatility Using Bollinger Bands and the Average True Range Indicator

Daily OEUR.JPY=R

Bearish price breakdowns

Prices hug lower Bollinger Band
as volatility increases

Volatility increase
pushes ATR higher

Source: Reuters

51

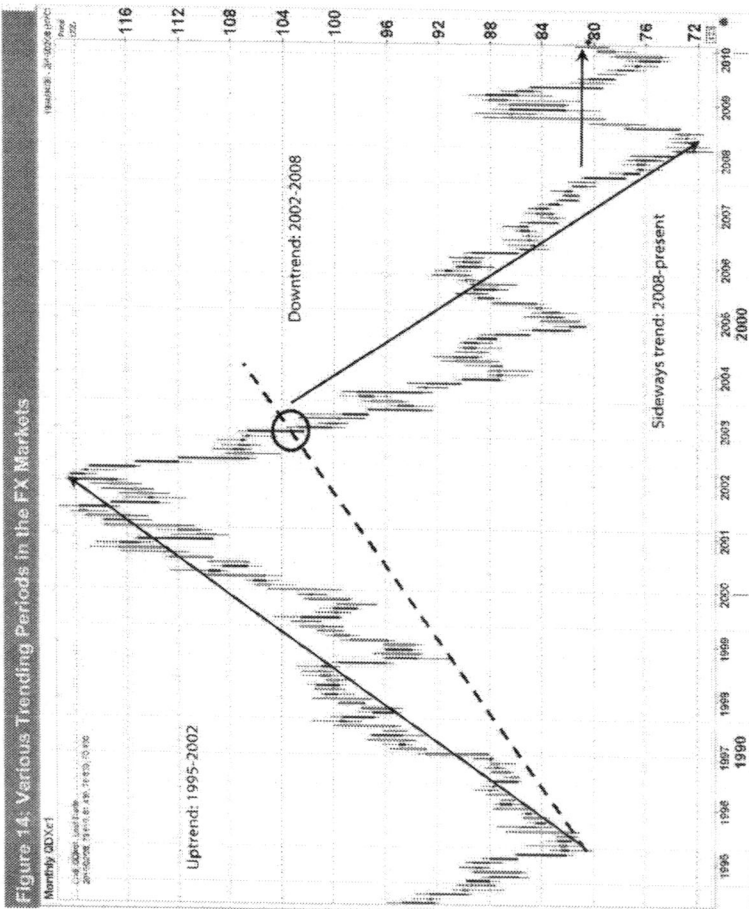

Figure 14: Various Trending Periods in the FX Markets

Uptrend: 1995-2002

Downtrend: 2002-2008

Sideways trend: 2008-present

Source: Reuters

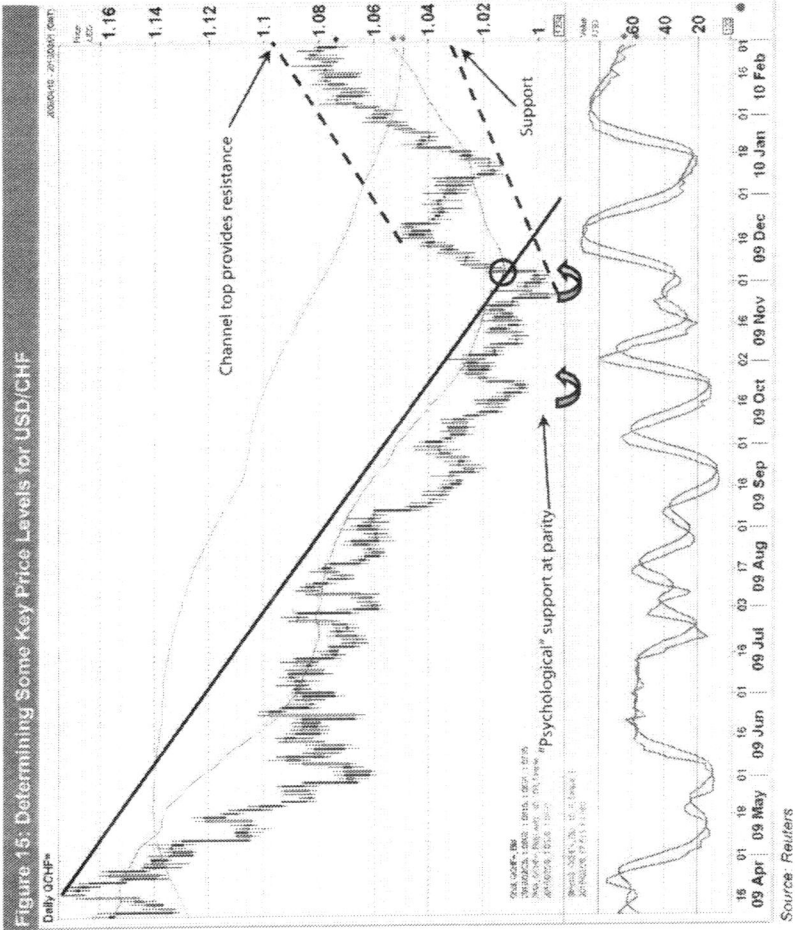

Figure 15: Determining Some Key Price Levels for USD/CHF

Daily QCHF=

Channel top provides resistance

Support

"Psychological" support at parity

Source Reuters

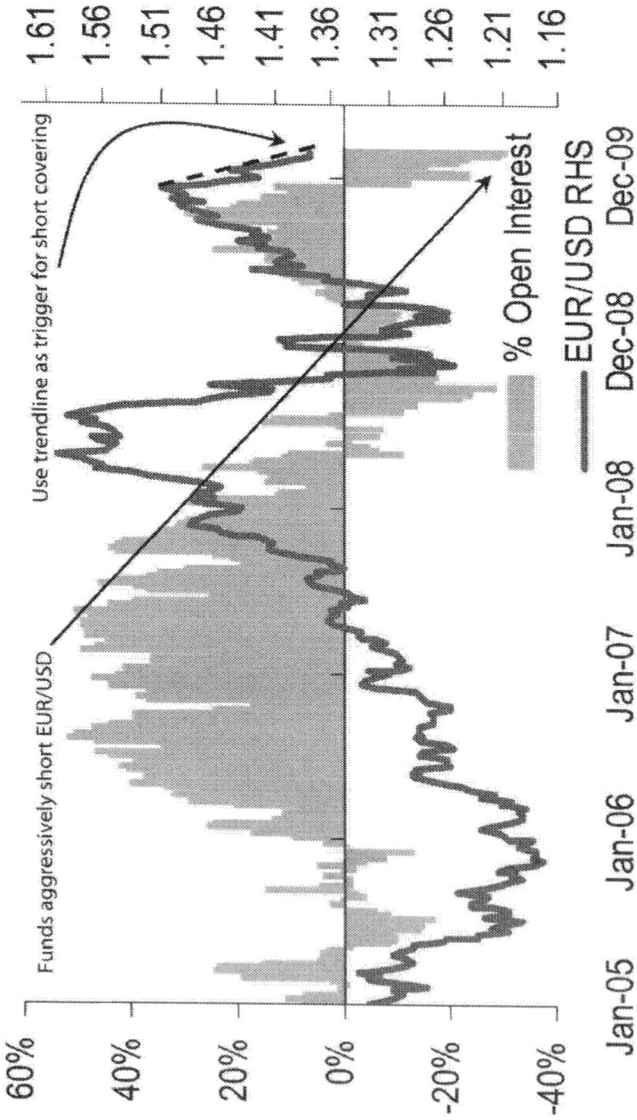

Figure 16: IMM Percentage Open Interest Data and the Effect of Funds on FX Markets

Source: Bloomberg, RBC Capital Markets

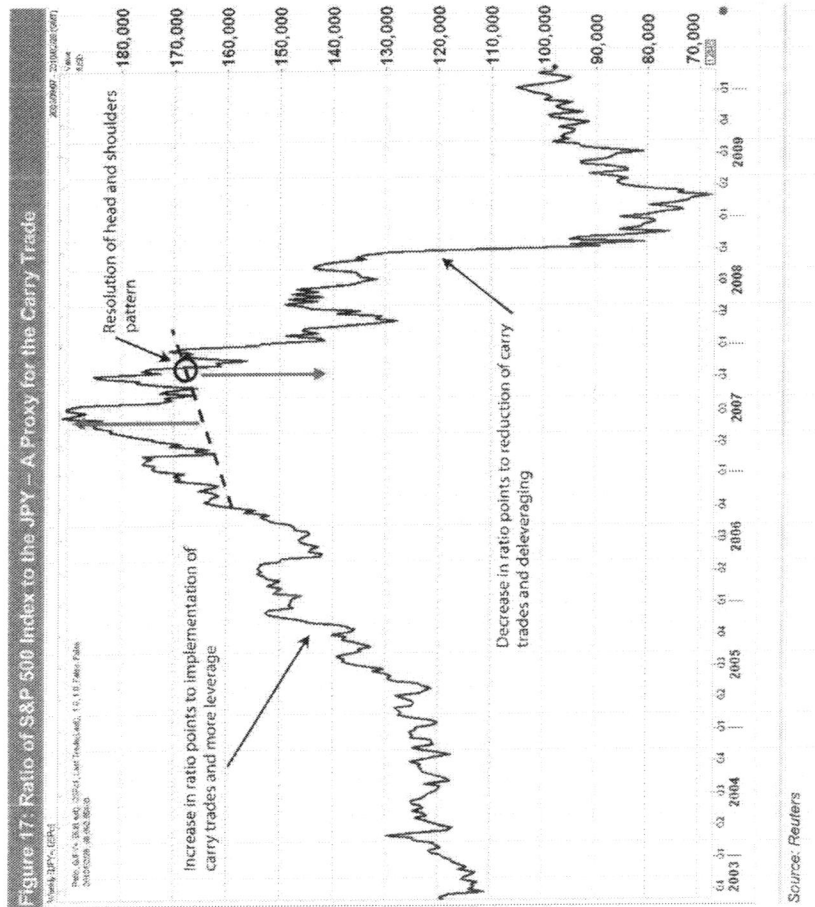

Figure 17: Ratio of S&P 500 Index to the JPY – A Proxy for the Carry Trade

Source: Reuters

55

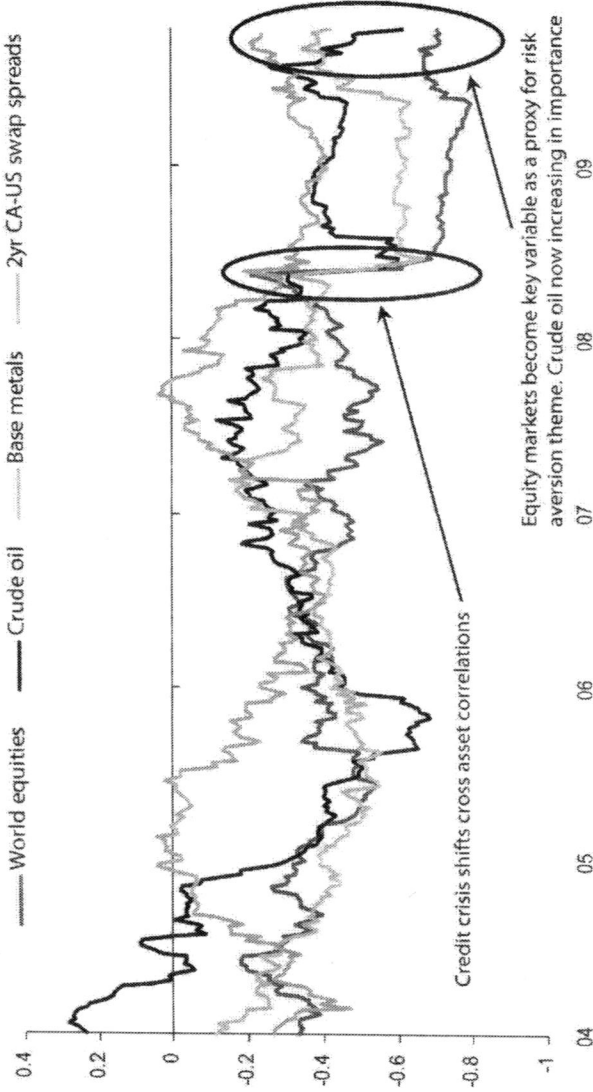

Figure 18: Cross Asset Correlations With USD/CAD

World equities —— Crude oil ······ Base metals ------ 2yr CA-US swap spreads

Credit crisis shifts cross asset correlations

Equity markets become key variable as a proxy for risk aversion theme. Crude oil now increasing in importance

Source: Bloomberg, RBC Capital Markets

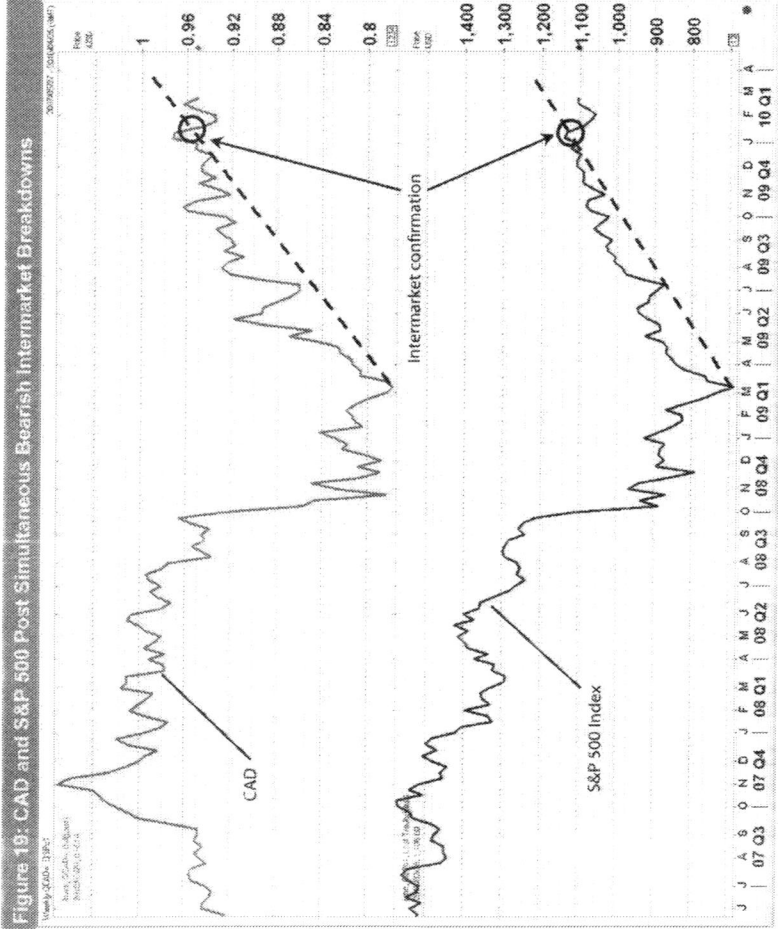

Figure 19: CAD and S&P 500 Post Simultaneous Bearish Intermarket Breakdowns

Source: Reuters

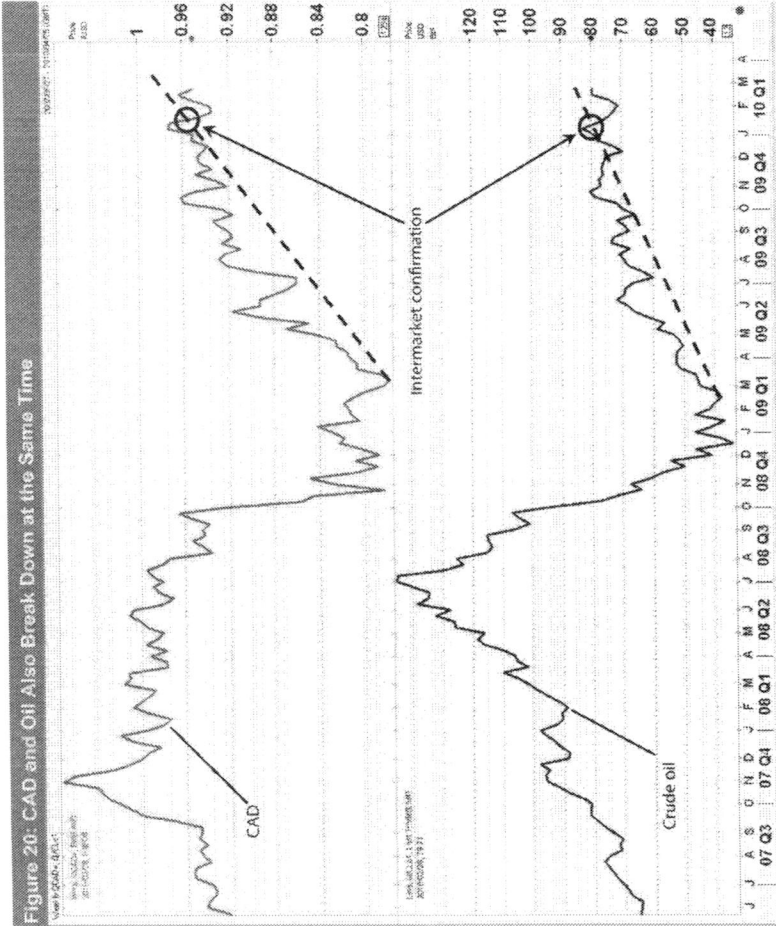

Figure 20: CAD and Oil Also Break Down at the Same Time

Intermarket confirmation

CAD

Crude oil

Source: Reuters

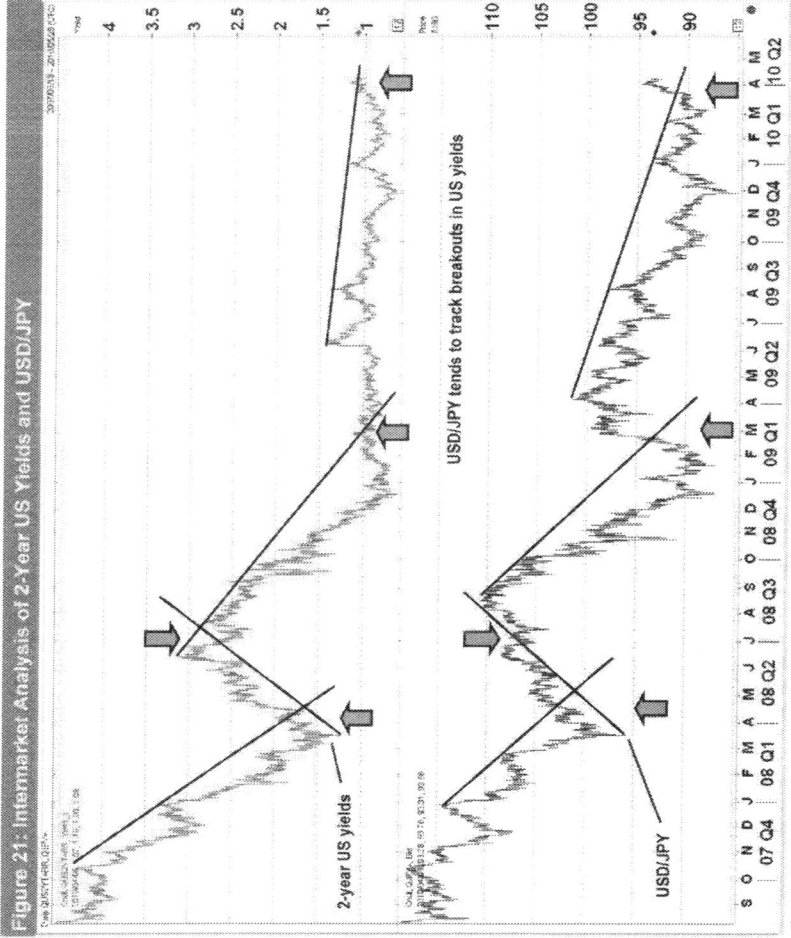

Figure 21: Intermarket Analysis of 2-Year US Yields and USD/JPY

USD/JPY tends to track breakouts in US yields

2-year US yields

USD/JPY

Source: Reuters

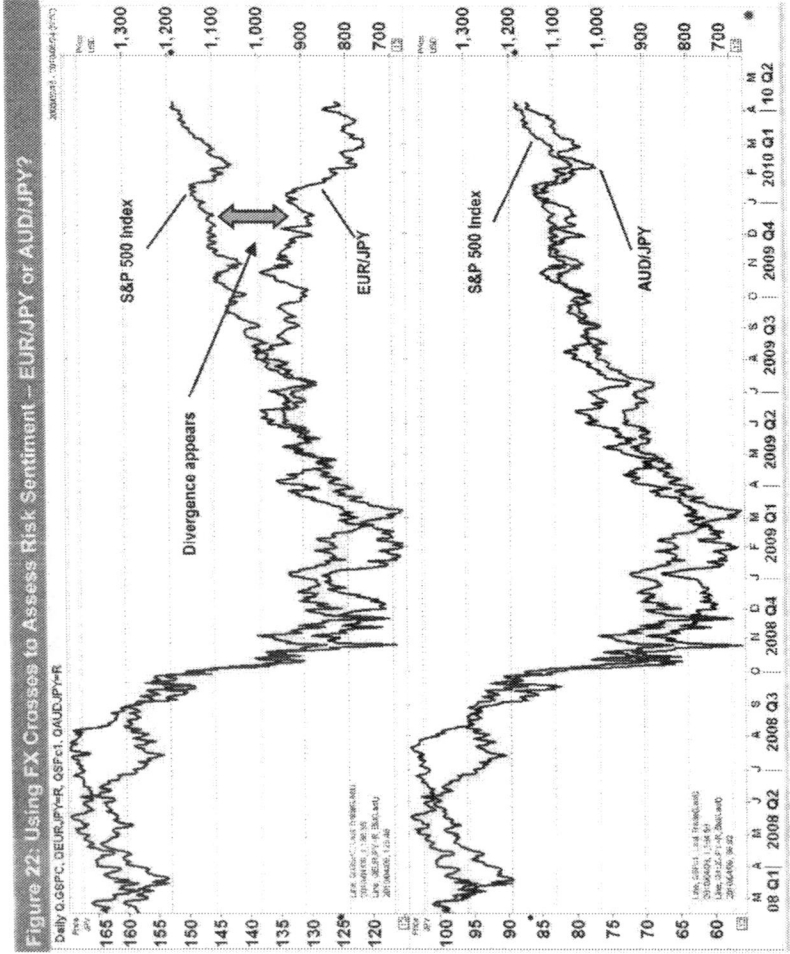

Figure 22: Using FX Crosses to Assess Risk Sentiment – EUR/JPY or AUD/JPY?

Source: Reuters

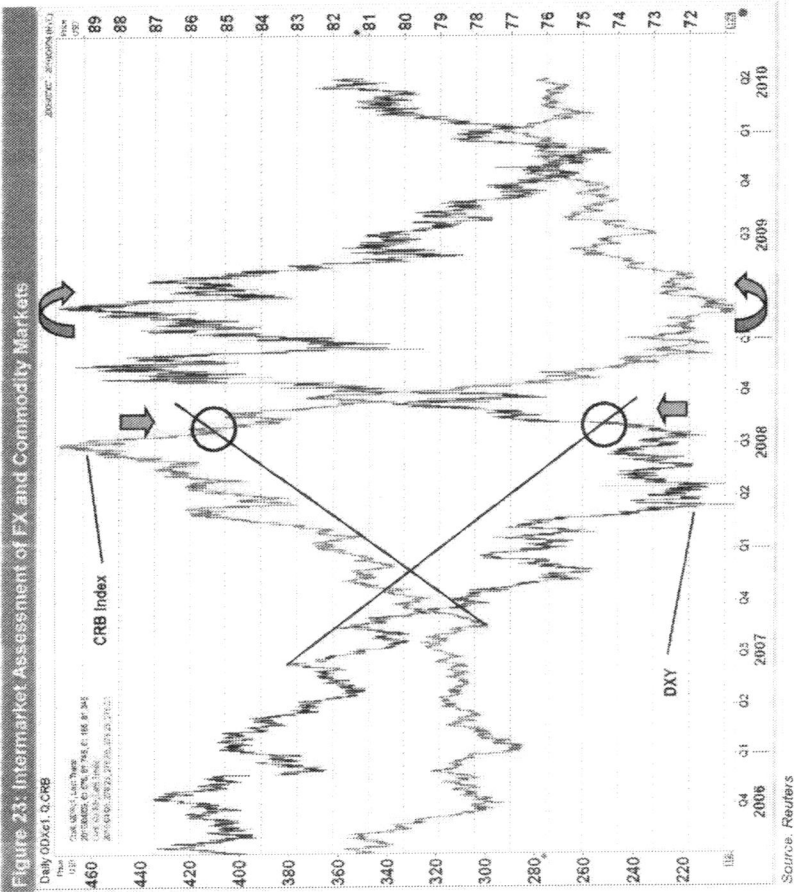

Figure 23: Intermarket Assessment of FX and Commodity Markets

61

Chapter 3

JOHN FORMAN

SENIOR FOREIGN EXCHANGE ANALYST
THOMSON REUTERS, IFR MARKETS

John Forman covers the FX markets exclusively in his role at Thomson Reuters IFR Markets in New York. Over the past 20 years he has covered all asset classes in his research since his career began at Thomson Financial in the early nineties.

USING TA FOR RESEARCH AND TRADING

Can you explain your basic research/trading style?

My research and trading styles are actually a little bit different. In my professional role as a currency market analyst I have to consider the audience and have to work within the general mandates of my position. That means I often have to take a fundamental view on things, not just a technical one. It also means that I often have to employ indicators and methods I personally do not use in my own trading for the simple reason that they are a common point of reference for my readers.

In my own personal trading and market analysis, however, I almost exclusively employ technicals. I consider myself mainly a chartist in that I focus on price movement and support and resistance. I do not employ indicators in any real fashion. I spent a considerable amount of my early years researching just about every one of them I could find, but in the end found they did not to add much value to my work. The only exception to that is looking at Bollinger Bands and Average True Range (ATR). That, however, is just about looking at volatility in two different ways – the standard deviation of price (Bollinger Bands) and ranges (ATR). I use them to help me identify markets or timeframes where an interesting transition in volatility may be setting up or taking place.

The question may come up as to how I can separate the fundamentals I track as a professional analyst from the trading I do as an individual. The answer really comes down to timeframes. As an analyst I'm very much short-term focused where my own trading is usually more intermediate to longer-term.

Which markets do you cover?

Generally speaking my daily focus is on a half-dozen currency pairs: GBP/USD, EUR/GBP, GBP/JPY, AUD/JPY, AUD/NZD, and NZD/USD in terms of technical strategy and analysis, and sterling in general from a fundamental perspective. Because of our short-term, often intraday, focus we have to keep things relatively narrow to ensure coverage when things are moving. As an analyst I have previously covered the equity and interest rate markets, and even done some short stints in the energy market. The result of all this exposure is that I tend to incorporate a considerable amount of cross-market analysis in my work.

How does your application of TA differ for short, medium and long-term time scales?

Generally speaking I use the same methods in all different timeframes. In my work I also mix in some proprietary studies which generally have daily or longer timeframes that are not as applicable intraday.

Do you think that the FX markets are more technically driven than other markets?

No I don't. The FX market, because of its size, tends to move more slowly in response to new information, but it definitely moves. I watch it happen every day both in terms of immediate events, but also in terms of lingering influences such as concerns about quantitative easing, expectations for interest rate moves, and risk aversion (to name a few recent major influences).

How 'random' or efficient are the FX markets compared to the equity or fixed income markets?

I think the FX market is probably the least efficient of the major markets because it defies clean valuations and arbitrages. Individual stocks and indices have easy and relatively direct points of comparison by which relationships and pricing can be defined. Index futures must stay in line with the pricing of the underlying component stocks, and vice versa. Individual stock prices are generally linked to each other in terms of relative valuations. In fixed income there are clear relationships between credit quality and maturities, and the differences between the pricing of different instruments.

Putting aside the required mathematical relationships between exchange rates (triangle arbitrage), the FX market is much more fluid and free form. There's no practical way to value a given currency on anything but the most basic macro level which makes such things of no use for analyzing short or intermediate-term exchange rate movement. That leaves exchange rates totally reliant upon the supply/demand relationship related to trade, capital flows, and speculative perception.

To what extent are the FX markets driven by sentiment? Is this possible to quantify?

The foreign exchange market is massively driven by sentiment, at least in the short to intermediate-term. Longer-term it's moved by trade and capital flows, but in the shorter timeframes perceptions weigh very heavily on price movement.

What are the best sentiment indicators to use?

There are two things I track to get a feel for market sentiment. One is the positioning data reported in the Commitment of Traders (COT) report each week. How traders are positioning themselves and actually putting their money at risk tells me more about what they are thinking than just about anything else. Granted, the currency futures market represents a relatively small amount of total volume, but it tends to capture the fast money fairly well, so I look to see when speculative holdings get extreme.

The other thing I keep track of by way of monitoring market sentiment is how price reacts to news. That is a real-time way of gauging the market's view on things and how it may be positioned. Obviously, though, this requires being able to stay on top of data releases, speakers, etc.

Does the application of TA differ when using it to analyse a currency index as compared to currency pairs?

In terms of general application, I personally do not look at anything different when analyzing an index vs. a currency pair. Having said that, however, it helps to understand how the index is constructed, as it can influence things considerably. For example, the US dollar index is heavily weighted toward the Euro. As such, movement in the EUR/USD exchange rate will be the strongest influence, by far, on the movement in the index. That means you can gain a bit more insight into what's happening by comparing the performance of the two to each other by way of looking for potential divergences.

Are there any market conditions under which TA works better or worse than other times?

Highly emotional markets which are seeing very powerful moves and very sharp turns (high volatility) are always going to present serious challenges to market analysis, technical or otherwise, because the actions tend to defy any attempt to classify or define them. From a fundamental perspective they make a mockery of any kind of valuation idea. From a technical perspective they make support and resistance irrelevant and shatter the idea of overbought or oversold. Of course on the flip side, very dull markets are equally as challenging for the simple reason that they just don't move. It's hard to make a profit when there is no price action at all.

Between those two extremes is where the markets mainly operate, but even in that primary range there can be considerable difference in methodology performance. I hold that changes in volatility are the main reason why trading systems experience varied performance. Some systems work best in low volatility environments, while others work best in more volatile settings. The experience of traders in recent years backs this up. The FX arena was unusually low in volatility in the years prior to 2007. As a result, a lot of low volatility strategies proliferated. When conditions changed as the credit crisis developed and increased market volatility, those former winning strategies saw serious performance degradation. No doubt many a trader took a big hit because they didn't recognize the implications of the changing market environment.

INDICATORS AND STRATEGIES

What is your reaction when the charts show a very obvious technical pattern such as a head-and-shoulders or a double top?

I don't personally focus much on classic chart patterns in my trading, at least not as they are developing and setting up entries. Because readers of my analysis do look at those sorts of things I will mention them when they appear. The one way I do use patterns like head-and-shoulders is to provide rough projections of where a move might take the market once the pattern has been completed.

How do you identify when a trend has commenced and may be nearing its end?

I use a basic definition of a trend as a sequence of rising highs and lows or falling highs and lows. With that as the foundation, when I'm looking for new trends that are getting started or existing trends coming to an end, I am looking for a change in the rising or falling highs and lows. Did an uptrend fail to make a new high or see the prior low penetrated? Those are indications of potential changing conditions. From a more trading system point of view, I generally use consolidation breakouts and breakdowns as signals of a potential new trend getting underway. Even there though, I tend to thinking in terms of the highs and lows when setting out my trend exit strategy.

What is the best method for measuring price momentum in the market?

I look at two things to gauge momentum: one is the size of the period bars. Are they getting larger, holding level, or shrinking? The other is the distance between relative highs and lows. As momentum fades the highs and lows tend to get closer together.

Figure 1 provides an example of what I'm talking about with the US Dollar Index during 2009. Notice how during the August to November period of the last major downtrend the lower highs were progressively closer to each other, as were the lower lows. That's a sign of a market where the major impetus behind the trend is waning.

Do you use Fibonacci, Gann or Elliott Wave techniques and if so, how?

I will sometimes reference Fibonacci levels or Elliott Wave indications in my professional work, but they are usually not among the first things I consider. I don't make personal trading decisions based on any of those three methods.

If prices reach a major support level do you wait until it has broken through before buying or selling? If so, by how much?

It depends on how I think the market is set up. If I am looking at an uptrend, and thus the move towards support is a pull-back within the larger move, then I would look to buy ahead of the support and probably put my stop below it. If, however, I'm looking to play from the short side then I would look to sell a move below the support point. As for how far below I put the order, its generally not much. I try to identify support and resistance points which, if broken, strongly suggest a change in the market's condition away from what I had been seeing.

How do you judge if a market is overbought or oversold?

If the market approaches important support and cannot go any lower then it is oversold in that timeframe, and vice versa for overbought. Alternatively, if there's been a very rapid and aggressive move in one direction and the follow-through is slowing down, then the market is overbought or oversold. I do not look to indicators like stochastics or RSI in that respect.

Can you give a chart example of an oversold FX market?

If a market cannot keep making new higher highs it is overbought; there's a lack of further buying interest. Likewise, an oversold market is one where new lower lows cannot be made because there is a lack of incremental selling interest to keep things moving.

CHARACTERISTICS UNIQUE TO THE FX MARKETS

How far out do you analyze the FX markets? What specific strategies do you use for longer-term analysis?

I will go out as far as monthly charts in my analysis, though for actual trading purposes I'm usually more in the daily/weekly chart timeframe. The chart and volatility analysis I use for my strategy decision making does not vary by timeframe.

Is there any difference in your approach between the analysis of G7 and emerging markets currencies? To what extent is liquidity in EM markets a factor?

My trading is pretty much exclusively focused on the G7 currencies, though I do have to look at the Latin American currencies in my work. Because they are often more thinly traded and can be subject to wider swings, I generally shift to slightly longer-term timeframes than I use covering the majors.

What fundamental information is most important for the FX markets?

It all comes down to things which will impact the value of a currency and/or the demand or supply of it. Inflation affects directly into the value of a currency as it represents an eroding of its purchasing power. Interest rates obviously speak to the potential for investment returns (though they need to be considered in a risk-adjusted and inflation-adjusted fashion). Money supply also suggests how much of a currency is available, with higher levels meaning less value per unit (which ties in with inflation). Anything which highlights the strength or weakness, now or in the future, of an economy will factor into things like potential return on invested capital and trade balances, plus some of the factors previously listed.

What is the best method of measuring volatility in the FX markets?

I look at volatility in two ways: one is in terms of point-to-point movement, meaning the volatility of closes. That can be tracked by Bollinger Bands which look at the standard deviation of closing prices. The wider the bands the higher the volatility as indicated by the standard deviation.

The other way I look at volatility is on a period range basis, meaning how far apart the high and low are on each bar. The Average True Range (ATR) study tracks this type of volatility.

On Figure 2, an S&P500 chart is plotted with the standard Bollinger Bands overlaid on the main price plot. Below that is a normalized version of ATR (N-ATR), which takes the standard ATR calculation and divides it by the n-period average, where n is the same number as the ATR look-back period (14 periods is standard). I use N-ATR because it is better for reference over longer timescales and across markets.

The bottom plot on the chart is the Band Width Indicator (BWI), which takes the difference between the upper and lower Bollinger Bands and divides it by the central moving average line. When you plot that you can see how the current width of the bands compares, on a relative basis, to historical norm. When it gets very low, in particularly, you have an indication that a new directional move of consequence can be expected to unfold before long.

Could you provide some examples showing how you use Bollinger Bands and the ATR to measure volatility in the FX markets?

Figure 3 is an example of how low band width preceded substantial moves in EUR/USD. Notice how the drops from 1.48 to 1.42 and from 1.42 to 1.35 were both set up by very narrow bands. Also notice two other things: one is that in the case of the third narrow band set-up there was a fake break higher before the market moved lower. That's always something to watch for. Often when it happens the reversal is quite violent, as it was in this example. The other is the way the bands stayed narrow for a while before the breakdown in the first narrow band set-up.

Figure 4 shows how the N-ATR can be combined with BWI to let you know when a market has a lot of pent-up pressure developing. Take a look at the combination of the very narrow Bollinger Bands and the very low N-ATR reading for the EUR/GBP weekly chart during the middle part of 2007. When this happens it means not only that a range break is setting-up, as the narrow bands signal, but that the period ranges can be expected to expand as well. Basically, it's a volatility double punch. The range which eventually develops is going to tend to be a fast mover.

Are the currency markets more or less prone to trending than stocks?

I haven't done any specific studies on the subject but my feeling is that in the short and intermediate-term timeframes, currencies are more prone to trend because sentiment is such a major force in currency pricing over those spans. In the long run, however, I think both markets are probably comparable in trendiness.

Are there any specific currency pairs that are more prone to trending?

While I don't have any empirical evidence on the subject, my personal view is that the JPY pairs tend to trend more persistently than others. The choppiest pair has long been GBP/USD, though I think the rise of the Euro has eased that somewhat.

What determines the 'key levels' in the FX markets?

As with any market, key levels in the FX market are determined by those doing the trading. They represent areas where market participants have either come to mass agreement on the value of doing trades (consolidation areas) or strong disagreement (rejection highs and lows). Of course there will always be points like trendlines and Fibonacci levels to which some folks attribute meaning. In the end, though, it's the market's action which defines which levels really matter.

Can you give a recent chart example of a consolidation area in the FX markets?

Three examples can be found in a weekly EUR/GBP chart (Figure 6). The first two are the horizontal ranges often thought of first when considering consolidations. The third one is a pretty massive triangle pattern which has been developing since the cross peaked at the start of 2009. Actually, we have a couple of classic chart patterns here. The middle consolidation is a flag, with the pole being the rally from the first consolidation. The big triangle consolidation could be viewed as a pennant, with the pole being the rally from out of the flag, though the size of the retracement might violate some rules there.

To what extent are FX markets seasonal? Can you give some examples of seasonality in the currency markets?

I have done quite a bit of research on seasonal patterns in foreign exchange rates and published a report on the subject entitled *Opportunities in Forex Calendar Trading Patterns* outlining my findings. The bottom line is that there are definitely times of the year when a currency or a currency pair tends to do better or worse than in others. Figure 1 again takes a look at the dollar in general terms. It highlights how the dollar performs throughout the course of the year based on 1-month returns.

What the chart shows is that during the early part of the year (the first 15-20 weeks), if you are long the dollar you do well. The middle part of the year is not a time to be long the USD. Then it's back to positive in the third quarter and mostly negative in the final couple of months of the calendar. While I can venture a guess that the dollar's early year gains are probably driven in large part by capital repatriation, I lack the specific knowledge of what in particular drives the seasonal patterns which show up in the FX market. It is, of course, tied in with major capital and trade flows going on during those times of year.

How do you measure the impact that fund flows have on specific currencies?

In the final analysis, the impact of fund flows on FX rates can only really be seen in the movement of those rates. Since there's no central information source, we can only guess at what the flows really are in any sort of real-time fashion. Data such as that included in the weekly Commitment of Traders Report allows us to look at flows in and out of futures positions after the fact, and that can definitely help see what has been going on in the markets, but that is only a fractional representation.

Is it true that currencies are especially susceptible to market rumours? If so, why is this?

I do not consider the FX market to be any more susceptible to rumors than any other market. There may be a wider array of rumours, but the size of the market necessarily means that on a relative basis the impact of them on price as compared to other markets is smaller.

Is the carry trade still applicable for some currency pairs?

As long as there is a sufficiently wide spread between the interest rates of two currencies, there will be those looking to do carry trades. Changes in exchange rate volatility (and that of underlying assets which would be part of the trade) will make carry trading more or less attractive, however.

How is the impact on FX rates of the carry trade best measured?

Without some kind of indication as to how much carry trade activity there actually is, there is no real way to gauge its impact on the market. The one exception to that would be the complete absence over a sustained period of any other kind of influences to move prices around, which doesn't come around very often.

Is it possible to differentiate between times when the market is being driven by speculators and by hedgers?

The bottom line is that unless you're working for a dealer who sees the big flows, you're probably never going to know what's driving the market at any given point in time. Sustained short-term price movement, however, tends to be more speculative and investment flow oriented, because those operators can make quick decisions. Hedgers tend to operate in the higher timeframes as their decision-making processes are slower.

How can inter-market analysis and cross asset correlations be used effectively when analysing currencies?

Inter-market analysis can be extremely useful in analyzing currencies. I always watch commodities, interest rates, and stock prices to see if one or another provides a leading indication, or a confirming indication, of what is happening in the FX market. It is often said that FX moves first, then fixed income, then equities. That is generally true in the intermediate and long-term, but often in the short-term the drivers vary. I have seen plenty of times when US Treasury rate action tipped off moves in the dollar. It takes time and lots of observation to have a sense of the wider picture, but if you do it, it can help in many ways.

Can you give an example of cross market analysis that you do for the FX markets?

Figure 5 combines the weekly cash Dollar Index and the S&P500 going back to early 2007. We've had a lot of different market conditions over that time span and the comparison of the action on the two charts tells us a story. The first thing we observe is that for much of 2007 (first slope line on each chart) the dollar was heading lower while stocks were mainly going sideways (though making a new all-time high in the processes). The steady decline in the currency told us something was going on that stocks were not yet reflecting. It was basically a warning sign. Eventually (second set of slope lines) stocks turned to match the performance of the dollar.

Things changed in Q3 of 2008. That's when the fear really took hold in the markets and the flight to quality shifted the USD/S&P correlation to a negative one. We can see how that played out through the strong dollar rally coinciding with the sharp stock market sell-off into March 2009 (third set of slope lines), and then when both turned the other way (fourth set of slope lines). Knowing that stocks and the dollar were strongly negatively correlated through the risk aversion/acceptance market psychology provided us with an underlying awareness which we could apply in the shorter-term.

Finally, toward the end of 2009, that inverse relationship started to come undone as both stocks and the currency began trading in the same direction. This indicated to us that things had changed again; that the risk on/off trade was no long the dominant theme. The new theme was one much more linked to interest rates, which tended to bring the two markets into positive correlation. As improving economic fundamentals would mean better stock prices and increased prospects for rising interest rates to make the dollar more attractive.

Do you keep an eye on volume levels and if so, how do you use them in your decisions? What is the best source of volume data for the FX markets?

I do not track volume information in any real sense for the simple reason that the available data lacks coverage. A very large portion of daily foreign exchange volume is in swaps, which will not show up in any volume reading. The various spot brokers and inter-bank dealers do not generally release volume information, so what we are left with is the futures market and trade in currency ETFs. Sometimes that data can be useful, but mostly I've only looked at it to see if there are any notable variations from the norm. So called 'tick' volume is useless as it doesn't represent actual transactions in any way, shape or form.

USING TA IN TRADING

Can you explain your approach to risk and money management?

I've got a very simple approach to risk management. I never want to put myself in a position where I can't continue trading. That means I tend to keep my exposures relatively small realizing that the way I trade, which is mostly trend following in nature, can produce runs of losing positions. Keeping my risks small allows me to suffer the inevitable drawdowns without risking ruin.

Is TA a part of your risk assessment? For example, do you use support and resistance as likely levels to which the market will head?

Absolutely; I will always look first at where I will exit a trade in a negative fashion (stop gets hit), which usually is going to be based on support/resistance analysis. I will then use similar analysis to get a feel for what kind of potential the move I'm looking to play has in terms of profitability. If I like the comparison I'll do the trade.

What are the key performance parameters you look at apart from return?

I don't get too caught up in returns. Since I don't trade for a living I don't need to make any performance marks. I just do the trades that make sense when they come along and let the returns take care of themselves. I also don't get too worried about win %, which is perhaps the most over-rated performance metric out there. I'll look at trade expectancy and drawdowns when comparing trading systems, but in gauging my own trading performance, I focus more on whether I'm following my methodology and getting in on the trades I should be in on – not missing ones I should have taken and taking those I should have skipped. By doing that, everything else tends to fall into place.

How do you decide on which position size to take? How much of your capital are you prepared to risk at any one time?

Depending on the timeframe I am trading, I will usually risk between 1% and 5% of my account on a given trade (at least that's my preference). I take relatively more risk with longer-term trades because of the lower trade frequency than in the shorter-term where trades happen more frequently. My position size is determined by my point/pip risk divided into the account risk I've set.

What level of drawn down are you prepared to tolerate?

This depends on the timeframe I'm trading. If my account falls by more than 10% I will generally take some time off. For the longer-term trading, I'll give it more room though I don't really have any specific target level.

How do you measure the degree of risk associated with each trade you make?

I take a strictly technical view in terms of individual trade risk. By that I mean I identify my negative exit point and set my risk for the trade based on that. On top of that, if I am running more than one open position I look to ensure I am not going to create excess exposure in any given area. For example, if I am already long the dollar in one currency pair trade (say USD/JPY), I will be cautious about entering a new position which would be long the dollar (short EUR/USD) and thus adding to my exposure there. That said, most of the time I'm only trading one position at a time.

Which trade entry strategies do you use?

I tend to be more of a trend following type of trader, so breakouts and breakdowns tend to be the main entries for me. I will, however, also use tests of key support or resistance levels during a counter-trend move to enter or add to trades.

Which trade exit strategies do you use?

Because I tend to be a trend follower, my exit strategy is mainly using a trailing stop. I do, though, sometimes use targets in my trading and so will look for signs of fading momentum when near a target to get out.

Figure 1: Lower highs and lower lows for the US dollar

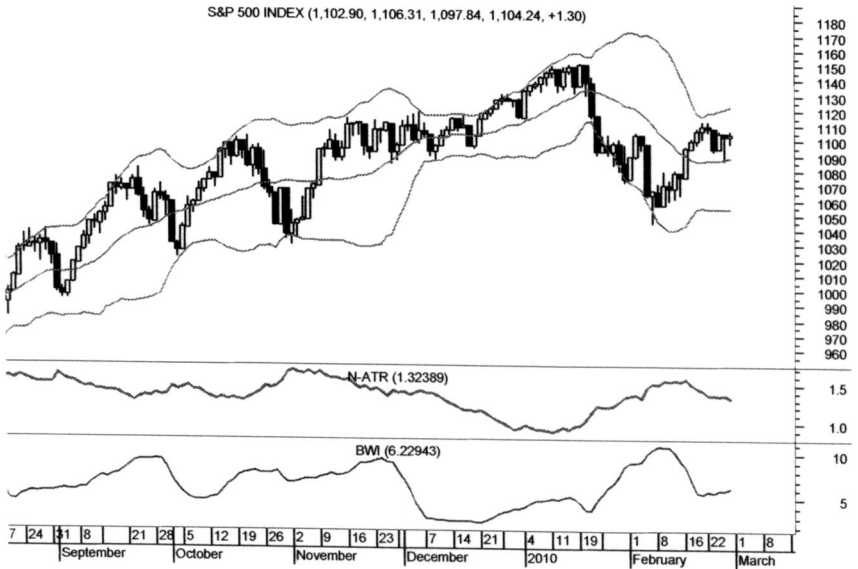

Figure 2: Using the ATR and BWI for the S&P500

FOREX EUR=,22 (1.3583, 1.3626, 1.3552, 1.3608, +0.0024)

BWI (3.30875)

N-ATR (0.95383)

Figure 3: Using Bollinger Bands for the EURUSD

FOREX EURGBP=,22 (0.8818, 0.8862, 0.8796, 0.8814, -0.0004)

BWI (5.36644)

N-ATR (2.01308)

Figure 4: Using the ATR, BWI and Bollinger Bands for EURGBP

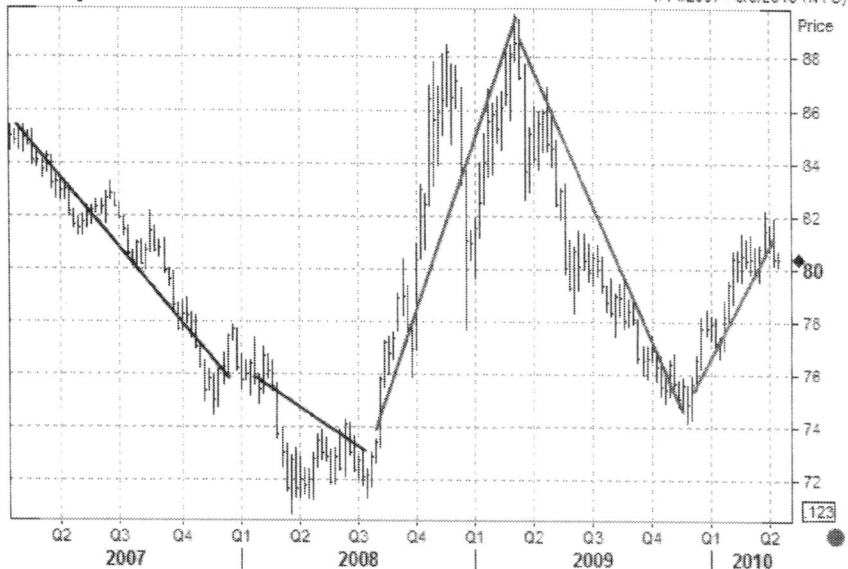

Figure 5: Combining the S&P500 and UD dollar index

Figure 6: Consolidation in EURGBP

Chapter 4

JEAN-CHARLES GAND

FX TECHNICAL ANALYST

SOCIETE GENERALE GESTION (AMUNDI GROUP)

Jean-Charles Gand has spent seven years as head of technical analysis at Societe Generale Gestion (Amundi Group) in Paris (formerly Societe Generale Asset Management). His research focuses on all asset classes but with a particular focus on market timing strategies. Previously he spent 10 years as co-head of the firm's dealing desk trading equities and equity derivatives.

USING TA FOR RESEARCH AND TRADING

Can you explain your basic research approach?

As a technical analyst for several years at Société Générale Gestion on the buy-side, I work exclusively for and with fund managers, fundamental analysts and strategists covering a wide range of assets. I edit a morning technical commentary as well as a weekly European sectors review, through strategic presentations based on intermarket analysis. I'm also involved in a long short equity fund, giving my opinion about pair trades and monitoring the short-term risk management. To summarize, my job consists of covering a lot of markets to help colleagues in their decision process to boost the tactical dimension of their investments.

I'm mainly concerned with European equities. Nevertheless, a technical analyst must study a lot of other markets to have an eagle-eye view upon the overall market environment. Intermarket analysis is a part of the body of knowledge in TA according to John Murphy. That's why I check the main asset classes like currencies, commodities, bonds etc. There has been a growing correlation between the equity market and the currency market over the past years. The difficulty consists in figuring out which market is the leader. Thanks to Robert Haddad, head of the trading room at SBA

(Lebanon-French Bank Group) and a top-gun technical analyst, my knowledge of FX has dramatically improved through the years.

How does your application of TA differ for short, medium and long-term time scales?

Because I work mainly for institutional funds and mutual funds, I adapt my research to fit with the mid-term perspectives of fund managers. However, if needed or otherwise requested, I might focus on daily and intraday charts. My application of TA is the very same whatever the timeframe as patterns are fractal by nature. In my view, the challenge is to jump constantly between different groups of participants, from day traders to monthly investors.

Do you think that the FX markets are more technically driven than other markets?

FX markets are highly driven by technical trading, much more than in other markets. Because of the strong trending nature of currencies, TA is particularly efficient and rewarding. It's no wonder that trend-following techniques have been the most applied in FX trading. I also look for situations when technicals and fundamentals are in synchronicity. Although my approach is mainly technical, I am not totally deaf to the economic and political releases and news that impact this market and all other markets.

How 'random' or efficient are the FX markets compared to the equity or fixed income markets?

Technical analysts believe investors have a propensity to act irrationally, driving prices away from the Efficient Market Hypothesis (EMH) true value. Because TA is the study of price action and knowing people set prices, I am quite confident that the big swings of currencies are neither random nor efficient as they are mainly driven by human emotions. I am a true believer of behavioural finance and I follow closely the research of Andrew Lo at MIT. I have hence adopted his very inspiring Adaptive Market Hypothesis.

To what extent are the FX markets driven by sentiment? Is this possible to quantify?

Sentiment, emotion or psychology have a major influence on price, creating trends and patterns because human biases, especially fear and greed, are the major trading system. Sentiment is obviously the utmost price mover.

Are there any market conditions under which TA works better or worse than other times?

There are no specific market conditions which make TA better or worse. I believe that a bull run, such as the 1995/2000 one, is ultimately boring for technicians whereas the subsequent bubble burst could or should have been avoided by prudent investors who master our discipline. On the other hand, 'black swans' normally stun everybody and are eventually hard to escape. I am thinking of the October 1987 crash.

INDICATORS AND STRATEGIES

Are there any indicators that work especially well in the FX markets?

It depends on the market condition. In a trending situation, I use moving averages. When I'm in a trading range, I look at supports, resistances, Fibonacci ratios and DeMark indicators, the latter being my favourite market timing tools.

How do you identify when a trend has commenced and may be nearing its end?

This question is about timing. My approach is based principally on DeMark indicators. In my view, Tom DeMark has developed the most innovative and powerful indicators of the last two decades. I was using them when I was a trader and use them now as a technical analyst because I haven't found anything as efficient in identifying exhaustion and potential turning points.

Do you use Fibonacci, Gann or Elliott Wave techniques and if so, how?

I use Fibonacci, retracements and projections. I don't use Gann because I find that it is too vague to apply robustly. I use Elliott Wave to identify where the market is in the cycle (impulsive or corrective waves), but I'm not an expert on Elliott Wave. I'm more confident in TD D-Wave™, a DeMark indicator inspired by the Elliott Wave method.

How do you use moving averages? If so, which periodicities do you use and do you use them directly to generate trade signals?

I use moving averages essentially as a trend following system. I'm usually conservative in the sense that my favourite settings are 200-days and 50-days because I want to see what the other market participants are seeing. Remember I'm not short-term orientated. I also have the possibility of using a moving average optimizer. This uses backtesting to work out which moving average type and period generates buy and sell signals when the price crosses one average or two or three averages cross one another.

If prices reach a major support level do you wait until it has broken through before buying or selling?

The FX markets are disadvantaged versus equities in the sense there's no information about volume. With equities, a validation of a major breakout/breakdown goes through a check of volumes. Moreover, as FX is more technically driven than other markets, traders know where the exit stops are and try to benefit from the situation. This means that investors can be easily whipsawed. Exits should always be placed at logical levels based on an analysis of trend, support and resistance, volatility and patterns.

How do you judge if a market is overbought or oversold?

Using classic indicators like the RSI is a popular way to evaluate extreme conditions. However, all indicators are only mathematical derivatives of prices. My judgement is more empirical. I mix a combination of sentiment barometers, DeMark indicators, the COT report, and measures of confidence to identify euphoria (when the market is overbought), and capitulation (when the market is oversold). As an example, Figure 1 shows the TD Sequential™ showing a '13' sell signal for EURUSD in 2008.

CHARACTERISTICS UNIQUE TO THE FX MARKETS

What intraday effects impact the FX markets?

I focus on liquidity and efficiency. Generally speaking, because the majority of major FX transactions are dealt during the US/European overlap, I tend to give more weight to price action during this time.

How far out do you analyse the FX markets? What specific strategies do you use for longer-term analysis?

Five to ten years are appropriate to have a helicopter view. Using the very same tools I usually use for equities, mainly medium and long-term moving averages. Trend lines and long-term supports, resistances and Fibonacci ratios are my other preferred choice.

Is there any difference in your approach between the analysis of G7 and emerging markets currencies? To what extent is liquidity in EM markets a factor?

No difference whatsoever. For emerging currencies, I recommend dealing when the specific market is active, due mainly to liquidity problems.

What is the best method of measuring volatility in the FX markets?

The Average True Range (ATR) indicator developed by Welles Wilder is based on trading ranges smoothed by an N-day exponential moving average (Figure 2). The Average True Range is a moving average of three true ranges: the distance between today's high and low, the distance between today's high and yesterday's close, and the distance between todays low and yesterday's close. As with all volatility measures, a high value tends to indicate uncertainty which can signal market lows (more often) and market highs.

Are the currency markets more or less prone to trending than stocks?

Currencies have the tendency to develop strong trends, stronger than stocks in my opinion because currencies reflect the performance of countries. The big picture doesn't change frequently based on a macro view.

Are there any specific currency pairs that are more prone to trending?

I would say exotic crosses exhibit important trends especially carry-trade crosses such as AUD/JPY, NZD/JPY and GBP/CHF to name a few. But since Q4 '08, we have witnessed with disbelief some pairs literally crashing such as GBP/USD, all GBP crosses, AUD and NZD.

What determines the 'key levels' in the FX markets?

In the long run, important international decisions, such as the 1985 Plaza Accord for instance. In the short-term, namely in intraday scalping, Fibonacci ratios seems to work perfectly well due to overwhelming followers that make me believe they are self-fulfilling. Round figures, double zeros and triple zeros are very important levels in all time frames.

To what extent are FX markets seasonal? Can you give some examples of seasonality in the currency markets?

Seasonality is a fluctuation or cycle forming a trend or pattern. In the FX markets, especially with the main currency pairs, the most obvious case of seasonality occurs in January (March in Japan) when foreign investors on the equity market and very big global corporations reassess their FX exposures and positions.

Is it true that currencies are especially susceptible to market rumours? If so, why is this?

Market rumours can have a significant and lasting impact on a currency until the facts confirm (or not) the rumours. David Furcajg, the founder of 3rd Wave Consult, did fantastic research about that point. Due to the large number of market participants, the liquidity of currency markets, and the intermarket relations, particular patterns may appear from time to time.

Is the carry trade still applicable for some currency pairs?

The monetary tightening process around the globe should weigh on carry trade activity over the next years. It is the differences in interest rates between countries which make possible such operations. In other words, a carry trade depends on spread. The Fed policy over the next months will provide better visibility on the impact the central bank policies around the world. RBA's recent increase in rates was the first significant example of the attitude of a central bank which doesn't want to suffer from an exodus of carry traders. Carry trades are also a question of investors' attitude toward risk. People having high risk aversion should not be willing to take chances with their capital.

How can intermarket analysis and cross asset correlations be used effectively when analysing currencies?

You have the everlasting negative correlation between gold and oil that continues to weigh on US dollar direction. Other on-and-off correlations can be found between equities/bonds and currencies. Therefore, when a correlation is clearly established, it drives your FX trading decisions: if gold prices are plunging, it is hence appropriate to buy USD.

Do you keep an eye on volume levels and if so, how do you use them in your decisions? What is the best source of volume data for the FX markets?

This is a specificity of the currency market: there's no definitive source of volume data. Because TA is based on the study of price action (price + volume), there's potentially a lack of information for the technical analyst. So I would look at the most liquid currency ETFs, especially in the US (e.g. FXE for Currency Shares Euro Trust Equity). Another way is to follow the buzz of some big market makers, such as Barclays and UBS that have the privilege of handing very big books.

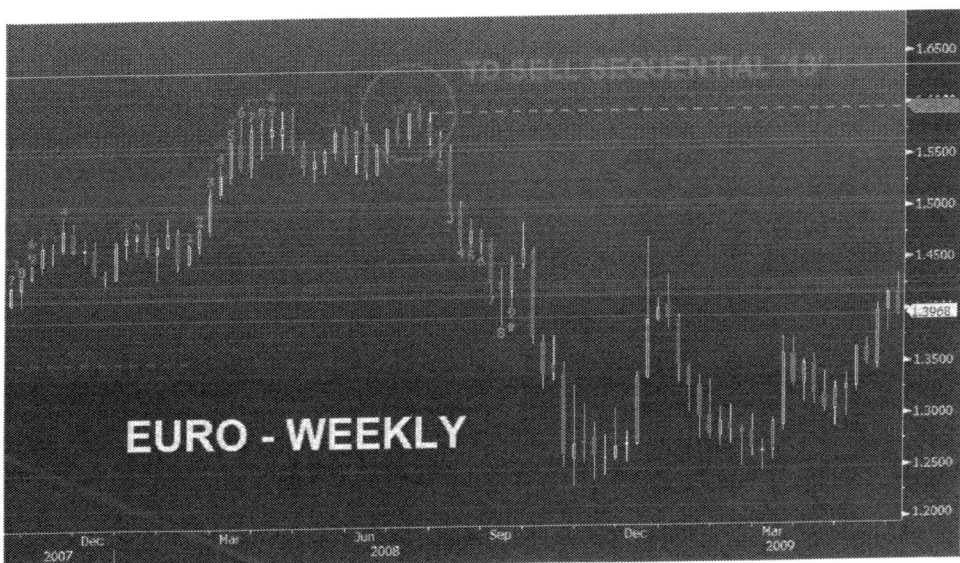

Figure 1: '13' sell signal for EURUSD

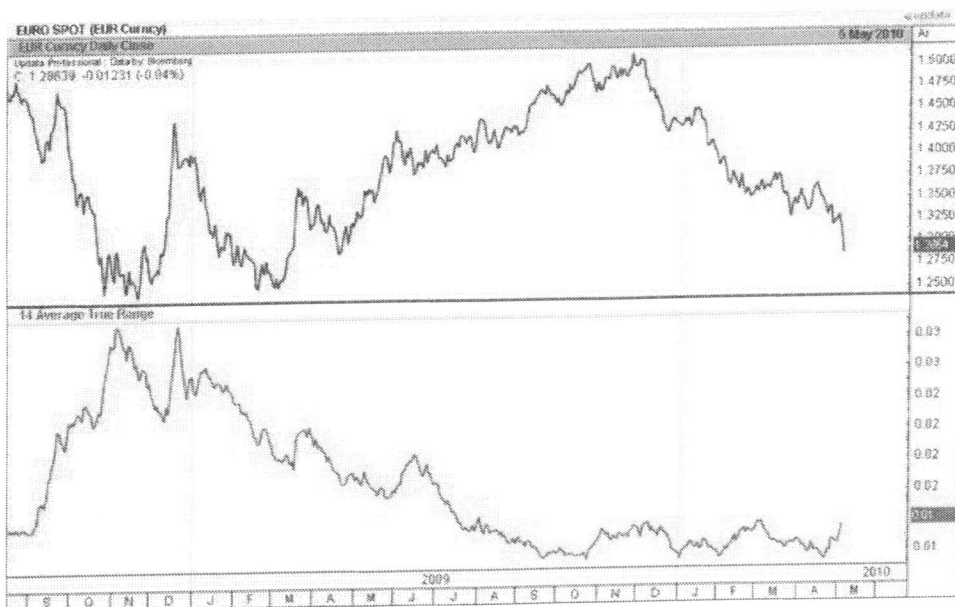

Figure 2: Using the ATR indicator for EURUSD

Chapter 5

CALLUM HENDERSON
STANDARD CHARTERED BANK
GLOBAL HEAD OF FX RESEARCH

Callum Henderson has worked for Standard Chartered Bank in Singapore since 2004. Prior to this he was head of emerging markets research for Bank of America and a senior emerging markets FX strategist for Citigroup, both in London. He is the author of four books on Asia and the global financial markets.

USING TA FOR RESEARCH AND TRADING

Can you explain your basic research style?

At Standard Chartered we take an integrated approach to FX research using fundamental analysis, technical analysis, flow analysis and medium- to long-term valuation. By themselves, fundamentals have only limited use. They can give you a clear story as far as a currency is concerned – whether it is likely to go up or down – but what they do not help with is *timing*. As the saying goes, timing is everything. Hence we use other short-term tools such as technicals and flow analysis to provide a more complete picture.

Within technicals, we do not look only at chart patterns, but also examine quantitative and seasonal patterns that are prevalent in FX markets, as well as between currencies and other assets such as equities, rates and commodities. With investors increasingly active across asset markets, the correlations between these markets have picked up considerably. As such, it pays to keep a very close eye on other asserts that may give important signals for where currencies might be going.

Valuation remains an important concept for us. To be sure, many of the traditional FX valuation models have a poor record over the short-term of predicting currency movements. For this reason we have developed our own shorter-term valuation models for specific currency pairs, which are particularly useful for the so-called 'emerging market' (EM) currencies. However, we also use some of the traditional models such as purchasing power parity (PPP) and real effective exchange rate (REER) to provide a more medium-term context to our currency view. At best, they are a reality check, but an important one at that.

Which markets do you cover?

As Global Head of FX Research, I run a team of FX strategists, which covers all the main EM and G10 currencies. Our core markets are in Asia, Africa and the Middle East, but we also cover G10, Emerging Europe and Latin America.

How does your application of TA differ for short, medium and long-term time scales?

We use technical analysis both for the short and medium-term views. Our application of these differs only in so far as technical analysis may be more of a primary driver of currency prices over the short-term in the absence of changes in economic data.

A further consideration is the 'microstructure' of the FX market. Estimates vary from 40-65% of total FX market volumes in terms of those that are purely driven by technically-related indicators. What is clear is that most systematic trading models use some form of technicals to guide their trading style. In addition, many FX overlay programmes use quantitative rather than qualitative indicators for this purpose. For all intents and purposes, this means technicals. If you add interbank and short-term traders to those two groups then it is clear that at least half the flow going through the market is technically driven. Most of the indicators used are three months or shorter. As such, flows and technicals in this segment are self reinforcing to a significant extent. This is not necessarily the case over the medium-term where other more fundamentally-driven market participants are present.

Do you think that the FX markets are more technically driven than other markets?

The consensus view is that the FX market is more speculative than other asset markets so one might conclude that it is more driven by tools or analytical frameworks such as technical analysis. However, there is actually little evidence for this – stocks, bonds and all manner of commodities all follow technicals closely to varying extents.

How 'random' or efficient are the FX markets compared to the equity or fixed income markets?

In my view, markets are neither random nor are they perfectly efficient, rather they are *human*. That is to say, market pricing is the result of a group of human beings analysing to the best of their ability (rather than perfectly) all the available data they can get hold of (rather than all information). Of necessity, there is a tracking error between theoretical perfection/efficiency and the reality. Put it another way, if markets were perfectly efficient, pricing trends could not exist. Supporters of the efficient market hypothesis (EMH), especially purists, should view the events of the past few years with considerable humility.

Market efficiency, whether in FX, equities or any other asset market goes hand in hand with other important concepts such as stage of development, liquidity and pricing transparency. Markets can be *more* or *less* efficient, but they are rarely if ever perfectly efficient. Typically, G10 currency pairs are seen as more efficient than EM currencies because of much greater liquidity, transparency and so forth. This is what you would expect from the EMH theory. Nevertheless, they can be subject to wild and volatile swings, which would suggest as well as extended trends, that all pricing-related information is not available all of the time and that the market has to play catch up as a result.

To what extent are the FX markets driven by sentiment? Is this possible to quantify?

FX markets are increasingly driven by sentiment. Quantifying this is next to impossible as the causes or triggers of sentiment are constantly varying. If we look at this from a balance of payments perspective, the original FX market participants, ahead of capital account liberalisation, were corporates. The opening up of national capital accounts has resulted in investment-related FX transactions, both those that are tied to an underlying and the majority that are not. Sentiment can affect all types of FX transactions, whether it is a corporate hedging their receivables, a central bank managing their FX reserves, a real money fund rebalancing their portfolio or a hedge fund shorting a currency. From a market perspective, sentiment is usually seen as a function of *risk*. As such, there are many so-called risk appetite indicators, which seek to provide trading or hedging signals for investors and corporates.

What are the best sentiment indicators to use?

We use our own model – the Standard Chartered Risk Appetite Indicator (SCB RAI). We introduced this in November 2005 with the specific purpose of tracking turning points in the FX markets. Unlike other risk appetite indicators, the RAI looks at the *appetite* rather than the *level* of risk at a given moment. We use for this purpose a mixture of both higher and lower-beta currencies and rank them both by the volatility of their excess returns and by the excess returns themselves. These two sets of rankings are observed on a daily basis. The basic assumption is that when the exchange rates that rank highly in terms of volatility also top the list of currencies that have high excess returns then the market's appetite for risk is also high. Similarly, the converse is also true. The RAI, which remains an index that is dedicated towards the FX markets, includes the following currencies: EUR, GBP, AUD, CHF, JPY, KRW, BRL, MXN and ZAR.

In trying to discern important turning points for the FX markets, we use both the daily reading of the SCB RAI and the 10-day moving average (MA); the latter is effectively a 'smoothed' version of the daily reading, which can sometimes be too noisy in terms of giving clear turning point signals.

Are there any market conditions under which TA works better or worse than other times?

Technical analysis works better in trending markets. When markets are choppy and trendless then TA can give many false signals which are subsequently reversed. From a sentiment perspective, this typically happens during Risk Neutral conditions – as reflected by our SCB RAI – rather than Risk Seeking or Risk Averse.

INDICATORS AND STRATEGIES

Are there any indicators that work especially well in the FX markets?

On the fundamental side, we pay close attention to economic indicators such as growth, inflation and balance of payments' data.

Moreover, the financing of the balance of payments, which links in closely with flow analysis, is crucial in terms of analysing FX market direction. On the technical side, we watch short-term momentum indicators such as RSI, stochastics and MACD, as well as key moving averages. We use 14-day RSI, which we find most useful in terms of timing the key turning points.

What is your reaction when the charts show a very obvious technical pattern such as a head- and-shoulders or a double top?

Well known technical patterns such as head-and-shoulders or double tops can be extremely important price setters over the short-term. As such, these may be a crucial reality check as to whether we should keep or reverse our short-term fundamental view. Granted, there are other important technical patterns, but these are two of the best known and as such most closely followed. We also look at rounding tops and bottoms as well.

How do you identify when a trend has commenced and may be nearing its end?

Determining the end of a trend is usually easier than the beginning – as typically you only see a trend confirmed some time after the fact. The end of a major trend is usually marked by choppy price action and a sharp increase in market volatility. From a technical perspective, this is usually reflected in a series of false breaks on both sides after a clear trend. Generally speaking, the longer the trend the more volatile the end of it.

From a flow perspective, it is generally assumed that genuine fundamental flows start a trend and speculative flows end it. When a trend starts, it is driven by valuation considerations of fundamental flows. Speculative and momentum-based flows join the trend, thus exacerbating it. However, at some stage valuation considerations change significantly causing fundamental flows to alter their behaviour – either selling into an uptrend or buying into a downtrend. In the short-term, this may not be enough to stop the trend. However, eventually speculative buying (selling) is overwhelmed by fundamental selling (buying) and the trend ends violently.

What is the best method for measuring price momentum in the market?

We use actively short-term momentum indicators such as RSI, stochastics and MACD. As with our usage of technical analysis within an integrated overall approach to currency analysis, we use the sum of the results of momentum indicators rather than individual momentum indicator per se. Figures 1-3 show how I have used the MACD to generate buy and sell signals in various FX markets.

Do you use Fibonacci, Gann or Elliott Wave techniques and if so, how?

We definitely use Fibonacci analysis for determining key turning points in short and medium-term trends. Typically, we see the 38.2%, 61.8% and 76.4% Fibonacci retracement levels as being more useful in determining such turning points. From a market perspective, you tend to find orders clustered around key Fibonacci levels, the triggering of which may exacerbate or reverse price trends. We also use Elliott Wave analysis for longer-term trends.

To what extent do you think that Fibonacci levels are self fulfilling?

To a major extent, much of technical analysis overall is self fulfilling. Because many people see levels as important, they therefore become important. That said, in so far as technical analysis tells the story of the economic cycle as reflected by price action, the analysis of price action through TA does have solid grounding. We use Fibonacci analysis a lot, particularly for longer-term moves. Typically, 38.2% and 61.8% Fibonacci levels are much more useful than 23.6%.

How do you use moving averages? If so, which periodicities do you use and do you use them directly to generate trade signals?

Many systematic trading models use moving averages for their trading signals. While one cannot generalise, these seem split into two camps: those who focus on certain moving averages turning up or down, and those who focus on breaks of certain moving averages. In the first camp, the 20, 30 and 50-day moving averages are very popular with trading models for generating trading signals. In the second camp, some models use the 32, 61 and 117-day moving averages, which are also Fibonacci numbers. From our side, we use moving averages, typically the 20, 30 and 50-day within our overall technical view. We do not use moving averages on their own.

If prices reach a major support level do you wait until it has broken through before buying or selling?

One cannot generalise. Support and resistance levels vary hugely in terms of their relative importance. We take a selective approach to the use of support and resistance levels. Key Fibonacci or moving average levels are of course incredibly important, as are record lows or highs.

How do you judge if a market is overbought or oversold?

In terms of technicals, we use momentum indicators such as RSI and stochastics. We also look at flows to determine whether or not the market is overbought or oversold. For instance, if positioning resulting from those flows is heavily skewed one way and momentum indicators are starting to turn against that, the market could well be overbought and ripe for a sharp correction. Our approach remains to use various types of analytical tools together in order to try and gain a more complete picture.

Which flow information do you use?

In addition to technicals we also look at flow analysis in trying to determine short-term moves in exchange rates. For this, we use our own flow data, along with Asian equity data. For Asian FX markets at least, the equity flow data is particularly useful as there is a high correlation between the equity markets and currencies.

CHARACTERISTICS UNIQUE TO THE FX MARKETS

What intraday effects impact the FX markets?

There are a number of important daily events, which impact the FX market. FX fixings can be very important in terms of order flow. In addition, regional centre openings – such as Tokyo, Singapore, London and New York – can affect market pricing because of the location of certain client types. Moreover, market views can vary significantly not only within, but between regions. For instance, you get periods in USD-JPY when Tokyo is a heavy seller of this pair due to trade or current account flows, but London buys it back because of speculative demand.

The most obvious example of intraday impact on FX markets is from economic data itself. Some numbers, such as US growth or payrolls for instance, typically have a larger impact on FX markets. However, the level of that impact is constantly changing, partly due to positioning ahead of the numbers and partly to changing focus within the market.

Is there any difference in your approach between the analysis of G7 and emerging markets currencies? To what extent is liquidity in EM markets a factor?

We do adjust to some extent the analytical tools that we follow to the market in question. For instance, technical analysis can be less useful in some FX markets that are either very illiquid or heavily distorted by regulation or central bank intervention. G7 FX markets are typically seen as more transparent, as well as being much deeper. Thus, they are seen as being more efficient, both in terms of the level of information that is incorporated in the FX price and in the speed in which that information is transmitted.

So-called 'emerging market' currencies have generally become more liquid in the last 10 years but remain subject to occasional 'jump' or 'event' risk. Local political dynamics have been much more important in determining FX market price action in emerging markets though they remain a focus in G7 as well. Indeed, with G7 governments now an active shareholder in the financial system, G7 politics is now more important for FX markets than at any time in the last 20 years. Overall, we try to take the same integrated approach – of fundamentals, technicals, flows and valuation for emerging markets as we do for G7 currencies, albeit with some slight nuances at the margin in emerging markets.

To what extent do you look at fundamental information?

We are definitely more focused on the fundamentals of the view as our starting point. After that comes technical, flow, valuation and increasingly quantitative analysis. Fundamentals cannot tell you the 'when' or 'how much' but they do tell you the 'why.' To us, it is the 'why' that is the most important factor in determining the direction of the trend. Fundamentals are particularly useful in determining divergence between economies and thus currencies.

If all information is in the price of a chart, why does analysing fundamental information add value?

Because all the information is not in the chart, since the chart is automatically backward looking. Neither does technical analysis have all the answers. That is precisely why one needs to combine the two to get a more complete picture of what is going on and even then, it is far from certain that one has a fully complete picture.

How do you combine the application of TA and fundamentals in your analysis?

We use fundamentals for the FX view and shorter-term analytical tools such as technical and flow analysis for timing the view. Technical analysis is very useful as a reality check for the fundamental view. Sometimes the technicals agree with the fundamentals – and sometimes they do not. When they do not, we go back and revisit the fundamental view to see if we have missed something. Longer-term technicals have a better correlation with fundamentals as they are effectively a function of the economic cycle. Short-term technical analysis deals with 'noise'. For that precise reason, it is very useful in providing major support to fundamental analysis, particularly when economics alone is not enough to give a short-term view.

What is the best method of measuring volatility in the FX markets?

FX markets of course provide their own measures of volatility in the form of implied and realised vol. This is useful not only for option traders – and clients that trade or hedge using options – but also for the rest of the market. The comparison between implied and realised vol is a useful measure for whether vol is cheap or rich. Moreover, depending on the 'risk reversal' or 'skew,' it may have important implication for the spot price.

The options markets have become an increasingly important factor in spot FX markets, which is why it has become important to keep an eye on FX volatility levels. Of course, there are other asset market volatility indicators such as the VIX index, which measures the S&P 500 implied vol, which are an important factor in FX markets.

Are the currency markets more or less prone to trending than stocks?

FX, like any asset market, can be prone to trending or to periods of trendless volatility, depending on the underlying fundamentals of the global economy. One cannot generalise that currencies trend more or less than equities as fundamentals change frequently. However, it has been proven that FX is less volatile as an asset than equity. As such, it has at least the potential to be more prone to trending.

Are there any specific currency pairs that are more prone to trending?

One simply cannot say because this changes all the time. For instance, the dollar-yen exchange rate has gone through extended periods of range trading – reflecting a lack of a trend – only for this to give way to multi-month trending. Similarly, the euro-dollar exchange rate has seen multi-month and even multi-year trends, only for this to give way to directionless range trading. Typically, G7 FX markets have been more prone to clear trends as they are less manipulated or distorted. However, with increased liquidity and market efficiency, the emerging market currencies now increasingly see longer-term trends develop.

What determines the 'key levels' in the FX markets?

'Key levels' are determined by technical analysis. Order clusters typically follow key technical support and resistance levels, thus becoming self reinforcing. In addition, the increasing importance of the FX options' market to the spot market, and more specifically the existence of large exotic option trades such as range binaries or double no touches, has created a different kind of 'key levels.'

To what extent are FX markets seasonal? Can you give some examples of seasonality in the currency markets?

Excluding crisis years, Q1 and Q4 are typically quarters that see higher levels of risk appetite while Q2 and Q3 typically see lower levels. With currencies increasingly linked broadly to overall levels of risk appetite and more specifically to other asset markets such as stocks and bonds, it should be no surprise that currency returns tend to be better in Q1 and Q4 against the world's funding currency, the US dollar.

However, this is of course only during times when the dollar is trending down. We keep a close eye on seasonality in our FX research. It is another tool in the box, but it is only useful as part of an integrated approach as with technical analysis. Past price action is after all no guarantee of what comes next.

How do you measure the impact that fund flows have on specific currencies?

We look at fund flows, both in terms of our own flows and flow information that is publicly available. Of the latter, the weekly Commitments of Traders report is the most obvious and well-known example. However, there are also other outlets for fund flows into stocks, bonds and money markets. For core emerging market areas such as Asia, we find the foreign flow data into and out of Asian equities (available on Bloomberg) particularly useful, not least as Asian currencies (outside of the Japanese yen) tend to be more closely correlated to equities than bonds.

With interest rates so low, we also watch money market fund flows as these are seen as a reflection of the appetite for risk. Heavy inflows to money market funds at a time of low interest rates typically reflect defensive behaviour by funds. As such, this tends to be positive for the US dollar and negative for higher-yielding currencies. Similarly, outflows from money market funds should boost other currencies against the dollar at the margin unless of course US interest rates are rising faster than elsewhere.

Is it true that currencies are especially susceptible to markets rumours? If so, why is this?

All markets are susceptible to market rumours to an extent. I am not aware of any research that proves whether or not FX markets are any more vulnerable to this kind of activity than any other market. What I would say is that the proportion of speculators in the FX market is probably higher than other asset markets. As such, the focus may be shorter term. Thus, on balance, currencies have the potential to be more susceptible to market rumours. However, on balance this is unlikely to be the case for any lasting period of time. The FX market is the deepest and most liquid asset market in the world. As such, it is also the most efficient. The impact of market rumours will swiftly and ruthlessly be eliminated if it is discovered that they are without foundation.

Is the carry trade still applicable for some currency pairs?

With G4 interest rates so low (spring 2010), the carry trade is definitely back in vogue. However, it is more nuanced now than just using a single currency such as the US dollar or Japanese yen to fund investments elsewhere. Policy interest rates in the US, euro area, Japan and the UK are 0.00-0.25%, 1.00%, 0.10% and 0.50% respectively. Interest rates in Canada and Switzerland are also 0.25%. As such, leveraged or funded investors – that is, investors who have to borrow to fund their investments – face a wide choice of possible funding currencies for the purpose of putting on carry trades.

However, it is not just the absolute level of interest rates that is important for carry trades. Two further considerations are FX market volatility and the direction of interest-rate expectations. In the first case, higher market volatility reduces the risk-adjusted return of carry trades. In the second case, higher interest rate expectations reduce the attraction of borrowing in funding currencies. We have seen this at times with the US dollar in the last six months even though policy rates remain at or close to zero. Until such time as we have inflation and a significant rise in interest rate expectations, carry trades should remain very much in focus for investors albeit that the choice of funding currency may vary over time.

Is it possible to differentiate between times when the market is being driven by speculators and by hedgers?

As mentioned, we watch fund flows very closely, both in terms of what goes through our bank and the available fund flow data that is publicly available. As such, there are definitely times when FX markets are more driven by speculators than real money funds/corporate hedgers, and vice versa. We compare our own data against that which is available publicly such as Commitments of Traders data, Asian equity flow data available from Bloomberg etc. At best this is just a snapshot of the whole, but it provides very useful information of which market participants are most active in driving the FX markets at any given time. While the FX market is seen as very speculative, typically speculators get overwhelmed by 'real' flow (real money funds and corporates) if they are out of line with fundamentals.

How can inter-market analysis and cross asset correlations be used effectively when analysing currencies?

We definitely keep a very close eye on the correlations between other asset markets such as stocks and bonds on the one hand and FX markets on the other. From a pure flow perspective, this is because many of the same investors are active in both stocks/bonds as FX. Moreover, FX is also impacted by the same fundamental dynamics to an extent. At times, FX markets are driven off interest-rate expectations whereby the correlation between swap spreads and exchange rates is high. At others, currency markets are driven more off equities. At times, FX leads and at others it lags the underlying asset markets. However, at all times it is worth paying attention to the correlation.

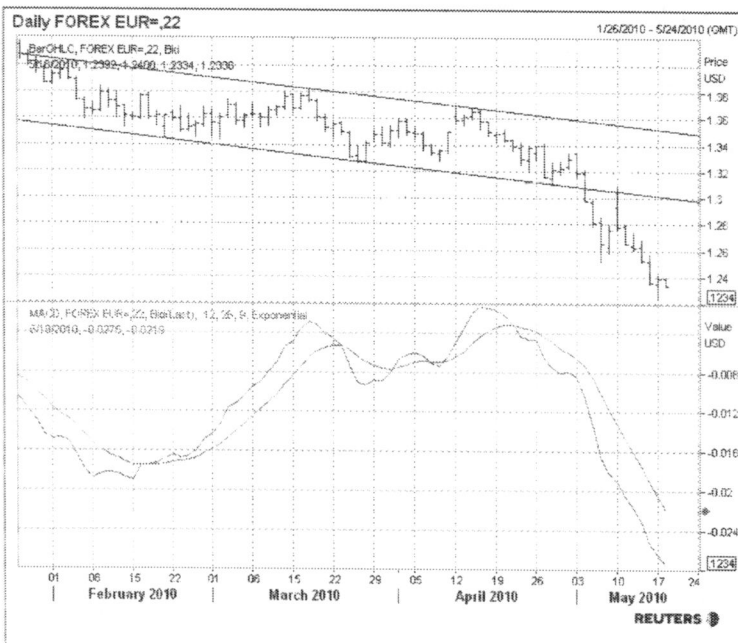

Figure 1: Using the MACD for EURUSD

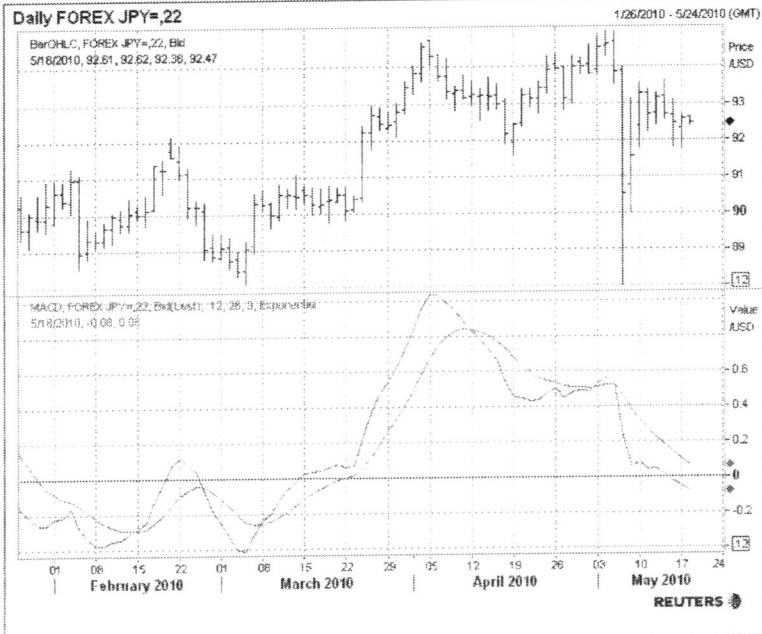

Figure 2: Using the MACD for USDJPY

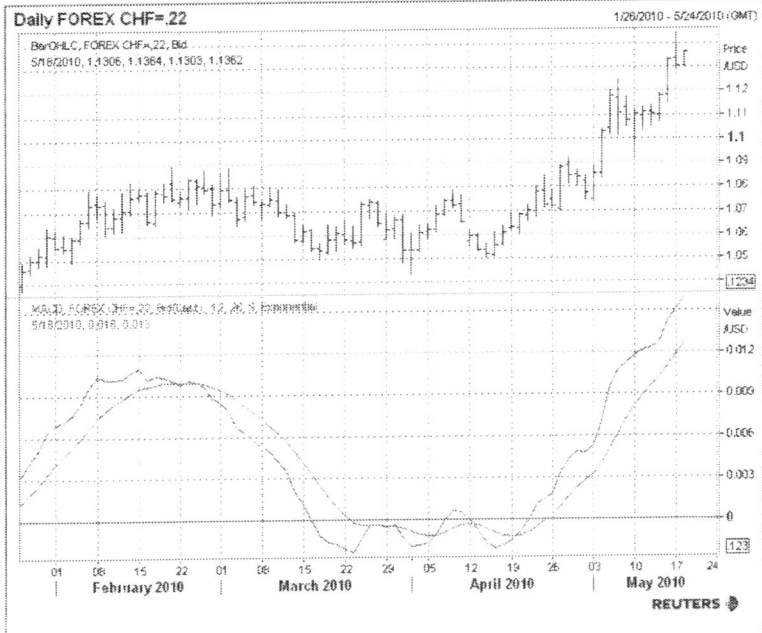

Figure 3: Using the MACD for USDCHF

Chapter 6

VERONIQUE LASHINSKI

SENIOR RESEARCH ANALYST

NEWEDGE GROUP

Véronique Lashinski is responsible for producing research on the FX and commodity markets at multi-asset broker Newedge in Chicago. She has over 15 years experience in commodity derivatives and technical analysis and is a board member of the International Federation of Technical Analysts (IFTA) and a member of the Market Technicians' Association (MTA).

USING TA FOR RESEARCH AND TRADING

Can you explain your basic research/trading style?

I write technical analysis reports for a leading futures commission merchant. My reports are meant to help the firm's clients fine tune or sometimes revise their strategy.

Which markets do you cover?

I primarily cover commodity futures and currencies. In particular, I look at the ICE Dollar Index (and its close relative, the EUR/USD), which has a major influence on commodities, the USD/BRL (Brazilian Real) for sugar, coffee and soybeans, and the CME British pound futures for cocoa futures.

How does your application of TA differ for short, medium and long-term time scales?

In futures analysis, you need to remember that you are making choices on continuations contracts when you look at long-term charts. When do you set up the chart to roll? What criteria do you use? Do you equalize or not? All these decisions can have an impact on the final chart. In some markets, the difference can be significant. I find that to be the case when seasonality is an important factor.

A long-term futures chart is a continuation chart because it is composed of the various contracts that have expired, but were at some point in the past 'the front month'. For example, a futures contract may have four months listed: March, June, September and December. So when you are analysing futures, you need to remember that you are making choices on continuations when you look at long-term charts. When do you set up the chart to roll: at expiry, following volume and open interest, or do you use a fixed number of days prior to expiry? What criteria do you use: volume, or are you trying to avoid major roll periods or deliveries? As futures contracts expire, there is often a spread left between the expiring contract and the next one. That is the 'continuation gap'. This is another choice for the analyst: do you keep this continuation gap, or do you remove it and equalize the whole historical data to the current front month? In some commodity markets where seasonality is an important factor, the difference can be significant.

Separately, I look at Fibonacci extensions, long-term price support/resistance areas on weekly and monthly charts. I find that support and resistance areas and trendlines are more approximate than on daily charts. Unless there is a spike for example and a very visible point that the whole market is going to be watching as a target, I use areas as opposed to levels on long-term charts.

Does the application of TA differ when using it to analyse a currency index as compared to currency pairs?

Perhaps because of my background and experience in futures, I find that my technical analysis tools seem to work best on Dollar Index futures. I like to compare the Dollar Index chart to that of EUR/USD as the weight of the Euro in the Dollar Index is 57.6%. When there is a difference, it could be an earlier signal.

Are there any market conditions under which TA works better or worse than other times?

I think there are times when different tools are useful, but it is rare that TA is totally useless. Technical analysis is a set of tools and it is up to us to select the combination of tools for the situation. If you can't drive in a Phillips screw with a flat blade screwdriver, it does not mean that you should throw away the screwdriver.

Here are some examples:

- In a fast move, the 50-day MA, then the 20-day MA may veer so far from the market that they are not relevant for a while.

- Trending tools are not meant for sideways markets. For example, using a long-term moving average for buy/sell signals in a sideways market.

- The use of the 'oversold' or 'overbought' concepts. The RSI is probably one of my preferred tools, but I am not looking for a price reversal just because the RSI printed 72.

INDICATORS AND STRATEGIES

What is your reaction when the charts show a very obvious technical pattern such as a head-and-shoulders or a double top?

I am weary of those patterns. They are widely recognized, even by fundamental traders. The risk is that there are many orders placed at the same place and so we end up with a fast whipsaw. I look for confirmation in the oscillator and in price action itself. In the case of a top, for example, if we have overlapping ranges and long upper shadows on the candlesticks, those increase confidence in the pattern. I prefer to either look at the shoulder as a sign of a top or wait for the return move and confirmation at that point.

How do you indentify when a trend has commenced and may be nearing its end?

At the beginning of a new trend, I look for signs of youth and impetuosity. These include long daily ranges with bullish candlesticks and few overlaps. The market should continue through resistance (or support, in the case of a downtrend) with ease. At the end of an uptrend, I look for signs of fatigue such as overlapping ranges, a flattening slope, smaller bodied candlesticks with longer upper shadows, and failure to reach the upper Bollinger band. Inter-market analysis is also useful here: if the market was following another and is now having difficulty keeping up the pace.

What is the best method for measuring price momentum in the market?

I like to use candlesticks and the RSI to gauge price momentum. I often put moving averages on the RSI or Bollinger Bands, and I look for M or W patterns. I also look for ranges to start overlapping and for the slope of the trend to become flatter. Those illustrate a loss of momentum and often precede a reversal (Figures 1 and 2).

Do you use Fibonacci, Gann or Elliott Wave techniques and if so, how?

I use Fibonacci extensions and retracements. In corrections, Fibonacci retracements are widely followed. Separately, how deep the correction is in relation to the prior move is a key indication of the health of the trend. For example, at the beginning of a move or if I think the trend is strong, I am expecting short-lived and shallow corrections. That is important, especially if I think it is the beginning of a major directional change. So I will look for the market to merely take a short pause then resume its fast move.

How do you use moving averages? If so, which periodicities do you use?

I mainly use them as support and resistance. I start with the 20, 50, and 100-day simple moving averages on daily charts because those are widely used and this is where we can expect resting orders are. On weekly charts I use the 13, 26, and 52-week moving averages which represent respectively one quarter, six months and one year. For Bollinger Bands, I use the 20-day moving average. Recently, I have used a 5% envelope on a weekly chart for WTI continuation support.

If prices reach a major support level, do you wait until it has broken through before recommending a buy or a sell?

In the case of a strong downtrend I would expect the market to continue below major support or produce a flag. A bear flag formation at a major support would not surprise me, but the key in a downtrend is that the bounce remains small. If it turns out not to be the case, this is an indication that the downtrend is not as strong as I thought (Figure 3).

How do you judge if a market is overbought or oversold?

I actually don't look at it quite in those terms. I look for M or W patterns in the RSI, and I use trendlines, moving averages, Bollinger Bands and look for divergences in the oscillator. I view those as a set up when things may be about to change. I have seen markets diverge for months before they actually reverse. The oscillator is a warning but confirmation will come from prices.

CHARACTERISTICS UNIQUE TO THE FX MARKETS

To what extent do you look at fundamental information? How do you combine the application of TA and fundamentals in your analysis?

You could say that fundamentals are the very reason why I look at particular currencies. As an example, commodities priced in US dollars become cheaper for an importer when the USD declines and more expensive when it rises. As a result, a lower USD is supportive for commodities priced in dollars, and a stronger USD is bearish on those commodities. So trends in the dollar are important in my work.

In the case of ICE cocoa and LIFFE cocoa, the ICE contract is priced in US dollars and the LIFFE contract is quoted in British pounds. The currency is a major component of the arbitrage.

Are the currency markets more or less prone to trending than stocks?

Currency markets trend and the usual tools work. However, I find that there is a substantial difference between currencies and other markets I cover. As a gross exaggeration, if my analysis suggests that a currency will double against another within a few months, I will stop and reconsider. Unless there is a major crisis in one of the countries, this is not likely to happen. A country's currency will impact the economy, its competitiveness and the attractiveness of its assets to domestic and foreign investors. There is a certain balance at play here. These impact the kind of trends I expect in currency pairs compared to commodities.

106

Figure 1: 'M' pattern on Bollinger Band for WTI Crude Oil. Source: CQG

Figure 2: NYMEX Natural Gas showing an M pattern on Bollinger Band.
Source: CQG.

107

Figure 3: NYMEX Natural Gas bear flag with the RSI and Bollinger Band.
Source: CQG

Chapter 7

EDWARD LOEF

SENIOR TECHNICAL ANALYST

THEODOOR GILISSEN BANKIERS, AMSTERDAM

Edward Loef began his career at Rabobank the Netherlands in 1985 before moving to Crediet & Effectenbank in 1998 where he served private clients with a special interest in trading and technical analysis. He has been at Theodoor Gilissen Bankiers since 2005 providing daily technical comments on the markets.

USING TA FOR RESEARCH AND TRADING

Can you explain your basic research approach?

My style is based on the principles of technical analysis and accepting that everything moves in cycles within a multi- timeframe span. So I've decided the thing I have to look for is some kind of technical alert that responds to the only constant in the financial markets which is change. Therefore I have built an automated technical model that applies some common technical indicators which answer the two main frequent questions asked: what should I buy and sell and when is the right time to act? In sum, my basic research style is almost mechanical now.

Which FX markets do you look at?

In my daily technical analysis I have a special interest in the daily trend of the Euro versus the US dollar. Of course I also look at other important currency pairs, but these other FX markets are most of the time a secondary choice for me, which just means a look on a weekly basis. This has to do with my profession as a Dutch technical analyst working in Amsterdam for a small private banking company. Most of the subscribers of my daily technical newsletter are private investors and traders or professionals in the investment advisory area and wealth management scene. Nevertheless, in my daily and weekly trend monitor I will be alarmed when buy or sell signals are activated. So I am aware of the short, intermediate and long-term trends in the currency pairs in the Euro, US dollar, Australian dollar, Japanese yen, British pound and Swiss franc.

How does your application of TA differ for short, medium and long-term time scales?

Looking at a 1-minute intraday chart of one trading day or an hourly chart of multi-trading days, I think the technical trader should be interested in only two questions: what is the direction of the underlying trend and when should I take appropriate action? I want to eliminate the subjective part of analyzing the chart so I prefer using pre-determined criteria. When showing charts in my newsletters, I use linear charts for short-term time scales and I prefer to use semi-log charts in medium and long-term time scales.

Are there any market conditions under which TA works better or worse than other times?

I think technical analysis is all about psychology. By the way, technical analysis is also very subjective. Fear and panic are much stronger emotional drivers than hope or belief. Under normal conditions one would expect prices to fall much faster in less time in a bear market than prices rise in a bull market. So, when stress is entering the markets one can witness sharp and clear impulsive moves to the downside. I think this is one of the main reasons why technical analysis is often only rewarded or popularized under bearish circumstances. This is when the outcome is far more predictable and which better suits short-term trader expectations.

INDICATORS AND STRATEGIES

What are your preferred technical indicators?

My preferred technical indicator would definitely be the directional movement indicator (DMI). I like the DMI because you see the strength of the positive or negative forces in play very clearly. The DMI also tells you something about whether the current forces are in the early stages or about to bend. So it gives me an edge in deciding whether to enter or exit a trade or position when I'm in doubt.

I use the DMI in combination with two simple moving averages (the 20 and 120-period) and the relative strength index (RSI), Figure 1. The only thing I'm interested in is finding which direction the market is heading and by how far. The averages, DMI and the RSI provide objective parameters for everyone interested in riding the trend.

What is your reaction when the charts show a very obvious technical pattern such as a head-and-shoulders or a double top?

Usually I get really excited to witness very clear technical formations with promising high probability statistics. Experience however has taught me to be careful about chart patterns which appear to be too good to be true because usually they are. If there's a lot of consensus among technical analysts then I tend to ask myself if this is a sign to go the other way.

How do you identify when a trend has commenced and may be nearing its end?

I like to measure the probabilities with the average directional movement (ATX) indicator along with positive and negative directional indicators originated by Welles Wilder. I look for ADX crossovers with positive or negative directional indicators when it's trading below 20. If this crossover is accompanied with a breakout in the trend I assume this is really worth take a further look at. I want to trade a trend from the left side of the rising ADX until a reversal takes place. At that time the odds are high the trend is about to bend especially when the ADX is trading above 40 and other technical indicators like the RSI is overbought or oversold. Confirmation is added when prices reach horizontal support or resistance.

What is the best method for measuring price momentum in the market?

One of the best indicators I'm aware of which I also apply in my trading model is the Average Directional Movement Indicator (ADX). I think it's one of the best methods because from a trading point of view I'm only interested in riding large impulsive moves. Check all your charts with large trending phases and look at ADX. It's a brilliant momentum indicator.

Can you provide an example of a recent ADX crossover in the FX markets?

On January 15th 2010 the 14-day ADX of EUR/JPY crossed above the positive DMI around 16 while the negative DMI advanced above 26 (Figure 2). This was an early bird sell signal at EUR/JPY 130.55. The buy signal to unwind the short position was activated on February 9th 2010 at 123.73. The 14-day ADX consolidated at 44 which is an extreme high in ADX readings. At the same time the 14-day RSI recovered from an oversold reading (Figure 3). This is an example of catching the trend as soon as possible when the odds are in my favour.

Another recent example in CAD/JPY saw a golden cross (a golden cross is a crossing of the short-term moving average above the long-term moving average) in the 20-day and 120-day simple moving averages on February 17th 2010 which called for a start of a bullish trend in CAD/JPY at 89.05. My trend following monitor combining the directional movement indicators registered a bullish momentum on March 16th 2010. The 14-day ADX went up and crossed the 14-day negative directional indicator while trading below 20. So, the uptrend activated a buy signal ('open long' position) in the early stage of the rising trend of the Canadian dollar versus the Japanese yen. On April 7th the positive directional movement indicator crossed below the ADX-line. This signal indicated to close the long position at 9360.

Do you use moving averages? If so, which periodicities do you use?

Moving averages are one of the best technical tools to show in slow motion what's going on. I combine two simple moving averages: the shorter-term moving average has a periodicity of 20 and the longer-term is 120. The trend is up when the price is above its 20-day moving average and this average is also moving above the 120-day moving average. The area between these two averages is regarded as a buying opportunity level.

The trend is down when the price is below its 20-day moving average and this average is also moving below the 120-day moving average. As long as this is the case, I would welcome any rebound above the 20-day average as a selling opportunity. Confirmation buy or sell signals are activated if the market price crosses the 20-day moving average in the direction of the longer-term moving average.

If the price reaches a major support level do you wait until it has broken through before buying or selling?

From a technical point of view, I regard a support level as a buying area and resistance as a selling area until these levels are broken by at least 3 percent or for two days if using daily data. Despite my subjective approach, I think a lot of buying or selling is triggered by computers.

How do you judge if a market is overbought or oversold?

I judge an overbought market with the RSI or stochastics in combination with the ADX indictor. In strongly trending markets, RSI or stochastics overbought or oversold conditions can last much longer than expected. To eliminate the risk of failure I want to know with the help of the ADX when the overbought or oversold conditions really matter. Multi-timeframe analysis should also help. I want to know if prices stalling near-term are providing opportunities to add to or hedge positions.

CHARACTERISTICS UNIQUE TO THE FX MARKETS

How far out do you analyze the FX markets? What specific strategies do you use for longer-term analysis?

My specific strategy for longer-term analysis is the slope of the 120-week moving average. I use the 20-week moving average as a trigger-line for a possible change in trend. So the slope of the 20-week moving average is also informative. The next step is to find out if there's a clear change in the process of tops and bottoms on a weekly basis. Pattern recognition and clear Elliott Waves add up to the weight of the analysis.

To what extent do you look at fundamental information?

I think fundamental information can be informative in stress circumstances, i.e. if the media spreads specific rumors about the weakness or strength of some currencies and emotional trading is likely to expand. Fundamental information sometimes provides a better understanding of the risks which is often useful to have in mind. Today, the recent widespread weakness of the Euro seems to exploit some fundamental errors made in the formation of the European Union.

What fundamental information is most important for the FX markets?

I think the difference between yields and macro-economic figures are the strongest drivers in FX markets trends. At least this makes sense to me if only I have to explain why trends change. But in the end it's all about supply and demand and I don't care much about the fundamentals.

What is the best method for measuring volatility in the FX markets?

Again I tend always to have a look at the height of the ADX indicator. But I also measure the difference between the highest high and lowest low over a specific amount of time. I'm using 20-period data and I combine these data with the (ATR) to catch the underlying trends and exhaustions.

Are there any specific currency pairs that are more prone to trending?

I think the Australian dollar and Japanese Yen against USD are prone to trending thanks to the search for commodities and developments in emerging markets and the need for exploration of oil.

What determines the key levels in the FX markets?

I think the key levels in the FX markets are highly influenced by Fibonacci retracements or round figures i.e. FX traders remember EUR/USD 1.60 in 2008 and EUR/USD 1.50 in late 2009 as important turning points.

Is it true that currencies are especially susceptible to market rumours? If so, why is this?

I think it is because we all know about the currency crises of the past (think of the British Pound 1992, Asian Currency Crisis in 1997 and Russian Ruble crisis in 1998). More recently, the Euro weakened rapidly at the end of 2009 and in the first quarter of 2010. I also think whenever the financial markets smell blood the sharks will be there to have their meal.

Is the carry trade still applicable for some currency pairs?

I think so but I would always focus on the charts to make up my mind about the trend and to make my trading decisions.

How can intermarket analysis and cross asset correlations be used effectively when analyzing currencies?

Since the USD plays a very important role in determining what the oil prices or prices of precious metals I make comparisons using correlation charts. Usually there seems to be some noise in the short-term, but the pictures are much clearer at longer timeframes, and overlays currencies, commodities, etc.

Do you keep an eye on volume levels and if so, how do you use them in your decisions? What is the best source of volume data for the FX markets?

As I said, my main focus concerns the technicals of the equity markets. I think analyzing volume is different in FX compared to equities. In FX markets it is for me almost impossible to keep track of all the amounts and sizes of contracts in a given period.

Do you think that the FX markets are more technically driven than other markets and if so, why?

I think so. This has mainly to do with the high liquidity of the FX markets compared to other financial markets. There are so many influences driving the FX markets that it is almost impossible to explain the cause of a trend or which factors are affecting the short-term volatility.

How 'random' or efficient are the FX markets compared to the equity or fixed income markets?

I think the FX markets are very efficient because of the amount of money flow involved. You need to have very deep pockets to influence the trends in the FX markets. For example, I can think of all central bank currency interventions in the past and still doubt if the underlying trend in the market was affected at all by them.

To what extent are the FX markets driven by sentiment? Is this possible to quantify?

Sentiment is playing a very big and crucial role I think. According to the Chicago Mercantile Exchange (CME), the recent speculation against the Euro led to a record number of open short positions in EUR/USD futures since the introduction of the Euro by the end of February 2010.

What are the best sentiment indicators to use?

One of the best sentiment indicators is the 'Magazine Cover Story" indicator originated by Paul Macrae Montgomery (Figures 6 and 7). The theory of contrary opinion analysis is best employed when weekly or monthly magazines publish a cover story associated with the financial markets. With hindsight this is very often a clear sign of a mature market crowd. I recall The Economist of February 7th 2004 calling *"Let the Dollar Drop"* and mentioning *"The Disappearing Dollar"* on December 4th 2004.

Other bearish cover stories like *"The Fall of the Dollar"* (The Independent, November 17th 2007) and *"The Panic about the Dollar"* (The Economist, December 1st 2007) all led to sharp countertrend moves in the FX markets. Regarding the massive short sale positions in the Euro, I mentioned in the last week of February 2010 that I wonder how long it will take until we will see another bearish sentiment cover story like that of 10 years ago entitled *"EURO CRISIS, Here's a way out"* (BusinessWeek, October 2nd, 2000).

USING TECHNICAL ANALYSIS IN TRADING

Can you explain your approach to risk and money management?

Generally speaking I reduce risk by trading in the direction of the trend. I don't chase the market but instead tend to buy on weakness if the trend is up and sell short if the trend is down as the odds are that the trend will resume instead of reversing. I only want to open long trades if prices show some kind of a bottoming process.

On a daily basis I look for a lowest low yesterday followed by a breakout above the high of the day before yesterday. I reduce risk by putting an initial stop-loss just below the V-shaped pattern (Figure 4) I'm looking for on a daily basis. I like V-shape bars both on the lows and highs all together in three trading days. The opposite approach is applied when the trend is down. From that very moment I trail my stops along any price move in the anticipated direction until my stop-loss has been hit. The maximum allowed risk should be 2% per trade of the total amount of capital monitored.

Is TA a part of your risk assessment? Do you use support and resistance levels as likely levels to which the market will head?

Absolutely since technical analysis is a great help in defining risk and reward by measuring the distance between the actual price, the nearest likely support level, and the next likely resistance. Trend channels also provide some insight into price targets in unchartered areas.

A buy signal or an uptrend confirmation signal close to support areas is very useful because I know in these circumstances very quickly if I'm wrong. If not, I ride the anticipated trend as long as possible. Charts show very clearly when the odds are in my favor.

What impact did the turmoil in 2008 have on your returns? What action have you taken to reduce any losses?

The turmoil in 2008 didn't come as a surprise to me. I recognized all kinds of important reversal patterns such as very impressive head-and-shoulders top formations in the equity markets. The statistics mentioned in *"The Encyclopedia of Chart Patterns"* by Bulkowski about this famous reversal pattern was really effective in foretelling the mess in the markets that one could expect to come. I went short in 2008 almost the entire year. I closed my short positions on the day's big headlines, when the media showed panic and/or pictures of imploding charts on their covers. I've warned the subscribers of my newsletters to pay special attention to risk management and stop-loss techniques all the way down. Because of the strong trending characteristics of the markets, 2008 was one of the best years in my entire career.

What are the key performance parameters you look at apart from return?

One of my most important key performance parameters is the win/loss ratio. It took quite a long time for me to build confidence in finding good entries. I need confidence to pull the trigger so I have developed the discipline of accepting a loss if it exceeds my risk tolerance. To keep the risk of drawdown acceptable, I don't want to risk more than 2% of the total account.

What annual return do you generally look for in your trading? How do you adjust this for risk?

My goal is an annual return above 20%. I think this is possible when using leveraged instruments and applying a trading style that is self-disciplined and uses proper position sizing. To adjust the risk I have to check and rebalance every day the open positions, raise my stops if necessary, and be aware of correlations between the assets in my portfolio. I like to have a focus. Hence, I manage a maximum of 10 open positions.

What level of drawdown are you prepared to tolerate?

I think 15% drawdown is about the maximum I would tolerate. This means in a hypothetical way, each trade is allowed to risk a maximum of 1.5% of the total account.

How do you measure the degree of risk associated with each trade you make?

Any time I open a trade I want to be sure the expected reward is at least three times the amount of the calculated risk. If I receive a buy signal and the support level is 100 pips below my entry, the next resistance should be over 300 pips.
Sometimes I have to ask myself if I would buy immediately above horizontal resistance if a breakout and big white candle is exposed. It pays to look at the slope of the ADX indicator if it's trading below 20 and it wakes up. If a strong uptrend seems to have started, I would use the lowest low of last three trading periods as a stop-loss to figure out if this is a high reward/low risk trade.

Which trade entry strategies do you use?

First I want to trade in the direction of the trend, so I tend to buy on weakness when the trend is up and sell strength in downtrends. My buy entry should show some kind of V-shape pattern. So I'm looking for a higher intraday low above the low of the previous bar. Confirmation to pull the trigger is a 'closing' above the 'opening' of this particular bar and a breakout above the highest high of the bar before yesterday. This kind of market action will help build confidence if the former bar was also trading in an 'oversold' area. The same holds true in the opposite direction. It's also important to be aware what the chart looks like in another timeframe. If indicators are oversold/overbought in a multi timeframe, I get really excited looking for setups of a major trend reversal. Bearish or bullish cover stories in these particular market conditions are a great indicator to go contrary.

Which trade exit strategies do you use?

I like trailing stop-losses adjusted for volatility. I apply 2x the ATR with a 20-period parameter. Every open trade should be closed if the risk-to-reward ratio has fallen to 1:1 and momentum is fading away. Another 'exit' signal could be triggered as soon as a black candle shows up after a so-called 'close long setup' (Figure 5). There's always another bus coming along to step into.

Another important consideration is when new entry signals are exposed in relation to existing positions. One should ask if this new idea has a better risk-to-reward ratio and/or improving relative strength compared to the existing open trades. The question about alternatives with better reward-to-risk ratio should always cross the mind of the technically oriented trader.

Figure 1: Using the DMI with the RSI   Chart sources: Reuters Metastock

Figure 2: An ADX crossover for EURJPY

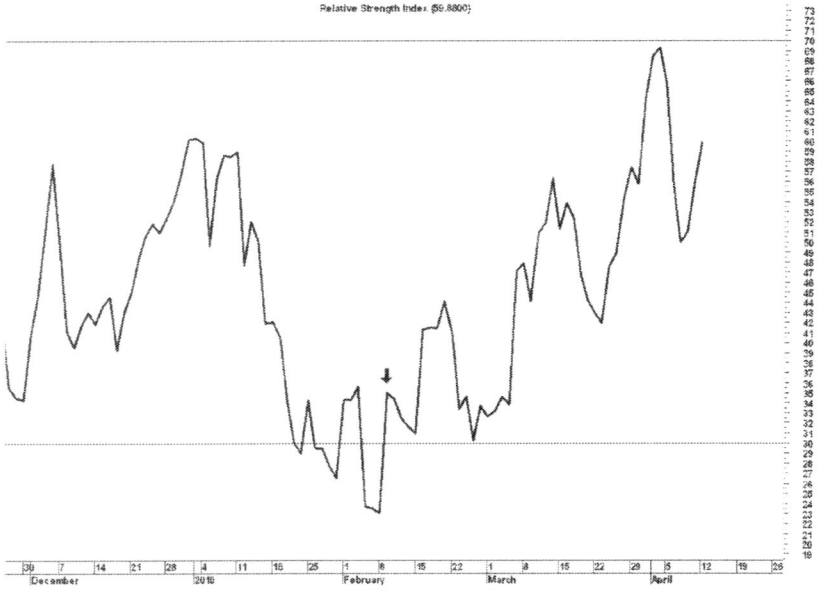

Figure 3: RSI recovering from oversold reading for EURJPY

Figure 4: Placing a stop-loss below a V-shaped price pattern

Figure 5: The Close Long Setup

Figure 6: Cover Story indicator - Business Week

Figure 7: Cover Story indicator – The Economist

Chapter 8

IAN NAISMITH

SARASOTA CAPITAL STRATEGIES

HEAD OF REASERCH

Ian Naismith runs SCS, an absolute return firm based in Florida that specializes in the use of exchange-traded and alternative index products. Ian also developed and co-manages the Currency Strategies Fund. Ian is the president of the National Association of Active Investment Managers (NAAIM) in the US, a large group that embraces technical analysis and tactical management.

USING TA FOR RESEARCH AND TRADING

Can you explain your basic research/trading style?

Completely technical; this encapsulates the collective interpretation and decisions made on the basis of news, events, stories, as well as fundamental and technical data. I prefer riding the noise to concentrate on the numbers. My trading style is a hybrid between momentum and contrarian methods driven by multiple technical models.

Which FX markets do you cover?

We look at all FX pairs - both majors and crosses. For our mutual fund, we measure European, commodity, and emerging market currencies against the US dollar.

How does your application of TA differ for short, medium and long-term time scales?

It is important to consider at least four different methods of technical analysis per time frame: contrarian, momentum, neutral, and a 'buy and hold' to verify all of the models' effectiveness. Then, from the present, apply a look back verification (generally within 20 rolling days) measurement to determine what model is performing best

124

considering real return, repeatability of returns, drawdown, and volatility.

It is the constant comparing of models that determines time frame. From a price standpoint, if a trader is using trailing stops and enters into a trade from a pre-determined maximum decline or maximum rebound, the greater the set percentage point (normally), the longer the elapsed time. Trading on the basis of price not time is an effective way to rule out noise. As an example, assume you are looking at price at 4:00 close on the NYSE today. Now compare today's close to the close 5, 10, and 20 trading days ago. The chart illustrates random periods of this simplest of indicators with the following formulas;

Short-term contrarian: 5-day rate of return of EURUSD < 0%, then long, if >0%, then short;

Short-term momentum: 5-day rate of return of EURUSD <0%, then short, if >0%, then long;

Medium-term contrarian: 10-day rate of return of EURUSD <0%, then long, if >0%, then short;

Medium-term momentum: 10-day rate of return of EURUSD <0%, then short, if >0%, then long;

Long-term contrarian: 20-rate of return of EURUSD <0%, then long, if >0%, then short;

Long-term momentum: 20-rate of return of EURUSD <0%, then short, if >0%, then long.

Model: compare the 5-day rolling rate of return of the above competing indicators, previous day RANK of #1 becomes 100% allocation for system today.

Can you give some more information on how your models are constructed?

That is difficult, because it is a system of strategies. However, generically, here is a concept that can help most traders with their trading: let's assume that a trader really likes 14-day RSI, 20-day exponential moving average, and the 20-day rate of return. They could create two different kinds of comparative analysis of each indicator. For the RSI, the contrarian strategy would be 'buy' if RSI closes below 20, and sell if it closes above 80; the momentum strategy would be buy when it crosses above 50, and sell if it crosses below 50. The idea with using it as a momentum indicator is that it could go from 50 to 80, remain between 65 and 75 for quite some time, then starts retracing to below 50. Those two interpretations of that indicator will give you very different results over time.

For the EMA, a contrarian method is buy when the closing price is below the 20-day EMA and sell when crossing above the EMA. The opposite would represent the momentum method. Obviously, these results will differ widely at certain times. Finally, for a 20-day rate of return method, the contrarian would buy if the last 20-day return is a negative, and sell when positive; a person using momentum would buy if the last 20-day return is positive, and "sell" when negative. Again, these are going to differ in results.

Now take the contrarian RSI, momentum RSI, contrarian EMA, momentum EMA, contrarian ROR, and momentum ROR and compare their respective returns for the past 20 days. These six return streams are literally competing for current use. The one or two strategies that are giving you the best results should be the strategy or strategies a trader should be using in their real-time trading. The reason is because many times markets will adhere to a strategy for an extended period of time before ultimately failing. As a strategy begins failing, the counter strategy will begin succeeding. The idea is not to stay in a failing strategy for too long, thus the look-back method will call you out of it and into the succeeding one before drawdown becomes too pronounced. Of course, there will be whipsaws between strategies, but generally the amount of decline is rather small. Imagine the examples above, except I use many more comparative indicators that are invented in-house.

Do you think that the FX markets we more technically driven than other markets?

I believe so. My interpretation of the FX market is that it is almost entirely technically driven. Most advisors I have met do not have much, if any, currency exposure, and many still rely on fundamental data or sentiment for stock or bond investing.

How 'random' or efficient are the FX markets compared to the equity or fixed income markets?

Compared to equity, and especially fixed income, I believe the FX markets are more efficient. Pricing flow and spike control seems more contained in FX due to the sheer amount of trading occurring in the FX market. That does not mean that the FX market is the definition of efficiency. There are many intra-day inefficiencies that can be translated into opportunities.

To what extent are the FX markets driven by sentiment? Is this possible to quantify?

I believe any market is driven primarily by three things: fundamental analysis, technical analysis, and the most psychological of them all – sentiment. Sentiment is the ingredient that can drive markets to their outliers (both positive and negative), can produce large ranging price cycles, or can even be the instigator of a trend that is detected through fundamental and/or technical measures. The FX market is not exempt. Other than tracking indicators that follow crowd psychology, quantification can be verified in a well executed system of models that capture moves in trades regardless of origin.

What are the best sentiment indicators to use?

Veering away from normal financial indicators, I believe the psychologist Elizabeth Kubler-Ross's model of the five stages of grief is a great indicator for bad trades and the partial inversion thereof for good trades. Specifically, in the bad trade scenario, if an investor is losing money, denial is generally the first reaction. Then anger followed by second-guessing and wishing for an alternative outcome. If the desired outcome does not happen, depression or apathy can set in. Eventually, the investor will accept what has happened and will consider adjusting their behaviour in the future. If enough investors are experiencing this simultaneously, the accumulation of similar emotions across the investment world is then reflected in the media to the point of absorption and definitely will show itself in technical oscillator indicators such as the Ulcer Index, RSI, CCI, etc. A disciplined trader is entitled to experience denial and even anger to the extent that they control the downside, but should avoid second guessing and apathy at all costs.

Can you give a brief description of the Ulcer Index?

The Ulcer Index is a measure of the stress level related to an investment market's behavior. It uses price retracements to measure "stressfulness." This is done by comparing recent price action with past price action. It was developed by Peter Martin back in the late 1980's. Unlike standard deviation, it is designed to measure the stress of drawdown. Many times, if the 14-day Ulcer Index has gone above 5 as a measurement, it could signify a good buying opportunity. It does behave similarly to the RSI, stochastic, and CCI etc. when interpreted as an oscillator. Peter Martin had a joke in the past, something to the effect that the higher the Ulcer Index of an item, the more you will be awake at night worrying.

Does the application of TA differ when using it to analyse a currency index as compared to currency pairs?

It can be similar or different. As an example, if a trader wishes to trade long the US Dollar Index (USDI) and is using the same technical analysis comparing the USDI to any singular currencies within the index, it is important they know how the components are behaving and to adjust the "short" effect the index would have.

As an example, 77.3% of the index is European currencies; if your analysis has you short the Euro and Swiss franc (which comprises 61.2% of the USDI) and long the British pound, Swedish krona, Japanese yen, and Canadian dollar (which comprises 38.8% of the USDI) - the trader would need to analyse the most efficient method to accomplish adhering to their model, whether it be through FX, futures, etc. Normally, trading the majors pairs in addition to cross pairs in concert is the most logical way to spread the risk.

Are there any market conditions under which TA works better or worse than other times?

It depends on the goal. If a trader is looking to make gains and is not pressured by comparison to a benchmark, then a trending market with minimal drawdown and low volatility is a desirable condition and requires little work. However, if a trader is pressured by comparison to an index, then they may be beaten because indexes can perform very well in those conditions. Technical analysis can give great results in volatile markets or in markets that move in either direction.

If a trader is using a contrarian model, and runs into a choppy market that favours contrarian trading, then rapid collection of positive trades can occur, even in a highly volatile market that is moving lower. Conversely, if a trader is in the wrong model in volatile markets, it can be quite painful. A rule that can be used is if a trader experiences a couple of bad trades in a short period of time that are outliers to their normal downside tolerance, then the sideline is a rational choice. Again, technical analysis is most effective in a system of models, so that when one model is beginning to lag against other model choices, it can be replaced with another model or models.

INDICATORS AND STRATEGIES

Are there any indicators that work especially well in the FX markets?

Most importantly, if "overthinking" and "underacting" were indicators, doing the inverse of those behavioural setbacks will help a trader succeed. The indicators or combination of indicators that a trader uses is immaterial if the trader makes a system so complex it cannot be practically used, or if a trader continually second guesses a good trading system. At some point, any indicator will work well. I don't believe there is a single magic indicator that can move through all market conditions and degrees of volatility without eventually exceeding drawdown limits. So having a competing system of indicators is the key.

How do you indentify when a trend has commenced and may be nearing its end?

I like using ratios. You can create a much more robust model by reducing indicator or price relationships to ratios. Generally, the ratios are using equal weighted multi periods of spread between two trading items and/or two indicators. Thus, if ratios are trending down to a sell signal (you can use a fast and smooth moving average such as Hull moving average to compare current measurement with recent measurements), normally you can sense in advance that the signal will be reached. But, do not trade with the belief that the signal will indeed confirm before it actually has confirmed.

What is the Hull moving average?

This was developed by Alan Hull, and his moving average is more responsive to current price activity whilst maintaining curve smoothness. The lag time for the moving average is virtually non-existent while smoothing simultaneously. I find it much more effective as a moving average than the simple, exponential or triangular.

What is the best method for measuring momentum in the market?

There are many ways to measure momentum in the market ranging from single moving averages to moving average combinations. Also oscillators like a self-adjusted RSI, stochastics, and the 20-day rate of return look back. The key is comparing indicators so that you create your own momentum indicator depending on which indicator is confirming its adherence to asset growth. In other words, many times momentum indicators can fail, especially in choppy, trendless markets where whipsaw trades can happen repeatedly, so have an indicator that also does well in those markets.

How do you use moving averages? If so, which periodicities do you use and how do you use them directly to generate trade signals?

Moving averages work fine as single indicators but a combination of moving averages can be more potent, such as the crossover of one moving average over another. As an example, with EURUSD a compressed weighted moving average crossing above a compressed adaptive moving average = buy, and crossing under = short; versus a compressed adaptive moving average crossing above a compressed weighted moving average = buy, and crossing under = short.

Compressed means within 5 days measurement. Historically, the compressed WMA crossing above (long)/below (short) the compressed AMA has been a great trade from the inception of the EURUSD pair, but as you will see in Figure 1, there are clearly times when the opposite will outperform if using a model look-back method. Also, fast moving averages (such as Hull) can provide a moving average direction. For example, if the Hull 12-day moving average direction is moving up, then it can hold a long trade until it has reached capacity, and short as the indicator moves down. Moving averages of indicators work well also, such as a moving average of price look-back, CCI, stochastic, MACD, etc. Any moving average timeframes are variable depending on the desired trade frequency.

Generally, compressed time frames of 5 days or less will result in less drawdown.

How do you judge if a market is overbought or oversold?

Overbought conditions tend to maximize on oscillators while minimizing on standard deviation. Oversold conditions tend to maximize on oscillators while maximizing on standard deviation.

CHARACTERISTICS UNIQUE TO THE FX MARKETS

Is there any difference in your approach between the analysis of G10 and emerging markets currencies? To what extent is liquidity in emerging markets a factor?

The same technicals are used for G10 vs. emerging markets. But, the volatility and correlation behaviour of each type of G10 currency grouping can be quite different. Paired against the USD, the G10 European currencies and Euro are less volatile and more inversely correlated to the US Dollar Index (USDI) than the G10 commodity currencies paired against the USD. The strong inverse correlation of the European currencies and EUR to the USDI is due to them making up over 75% of the index.

The Japanese yen paired against the USD floats in and out of correlation with the USDI. So, the G10 can be looked at as three trading groups. The emerging market currencies against the USD move in and out of correlation with each other and exhibit more composite volatility than the G10 European or G10 commodity currencies. All of these moving parts shifting in and out of correlation with one another, and being applied in the same technical framework, provides for smoother portfolio performance. Liquidity in the emerging market currencies has not been an issue as we trade emerging market ETFs.

To what extent do you look at fundamental information?

Very little due to its psychological bias. While fundamental data and sentiment are often the driving force of currencies, the confirmation of trading activity from fundamental or sentimental forces are more important via technical analysis. Again, fundamental information gives the fundamental analyst the strength for forecasting, and if correct, many times that analyst will successfully catch trends.

However, in my experience, those who forecast get caught in the "hold even if you are wrong" mentality in the hope of the forecast coming true. The technicals confirm the price effect of opinions derived from fundamental thinking.

What is the best method of measuring volatility in the FX markets?

The ratio of current volatility, such as 10-day standard deviation compared to a moving average of volatility (10-period moving average), can give a look at a possible future. Our firm exited more volatile currencies in August 2008 because of negative price direction compared to the US Dollar Index and volatility spiking of this ratio. More importantly, the ratio remained elevated and kept us from re-entering into a devastating situation for many currencies as 2008 began unravelling in the 4th quarter.

Are the currency markets more or less prone to trending than stocks?

It depends on the chart and currency pair you are looking at. If you look at a monthly chart with a 20-period moving average to define a trend, you'd be surprised to find that the EURUSD (most liquid pair) will breach the moving average more often than the Russell 2000. Since the phenomenon of high correlation between non-US dollar trade and the US equity markets took hold in 2003, the trends are very similar in length if measured monthly. However, weekly and daily charts tell a different story.

A weekly or daily measurement with a 20-period moving average will reveal that currencies will hold a trend over a longer period of time. In short, if someone wants asset class diversification and wants to keep trading to a minimum, reading weekly charts across the asset classes will give a more non-correlated portfolio.

Are there any specific currency pairs that are more prone to trending?

Over the last several years, the major pairs have held closer to trend than the cross pairs. Examples in declining adherence are EURUSD, AUSUSD, USDCAD, and USDCHF.

What determines the 'key levels' in the FX markets?

Significant support and resistance levels and mathematical landmarks (generally Fibonacci) within the support/resistance channel. Many view a single outlier bar up or down in a time frame as the absolute support/resistance, with smaller intervals being key through the consistent repetitiveness of bars touching similar levels. An example is a price bar stalling five times at a similar resistance value over a 50-day period on a daily chart.

To what extent are FX markets seasonal? Can you give some examples of seasonality in the currency markets?
Seasonal forces have been occurring in currencies for quite a while. The question is, can we plan a trade now with the expectation that the EUR will rally against the USD from the months of March to September of 2012 after it was walloped in 2008. What if the EUR doesn't exist in 2012? What lessons did the equity seasonal traders learn between 2000 and 2009? That holding on to a losing trade with the belief that the season will correct the damage doesn't make much sense.

Is it true that currencies are especially susceptible to market rumours? If so, why is this?
That can certainly happen, and increase short-term volatility. Another impact is the notion of 'connotation', meaning currently Greece is the "G" is the acronym PIGS. Has that psychologically impacted trading? You bet. Is the connotation itself a rumour? Maybe not, but it does create a general negative perception that spreads across swathes of traders who may or may not understand the reasons or motivations behind the acronym.

Is the carry trade still applicable for some currency pairs?
It has been a consistently solid strategy for quite some time, dividing up the G10 and trading the higher yielding currencies long against the lower yielding currencies short. However, keep in mind this strategy can be quite nasty if it unwinds. The strategy is a major source of financial liquidity in the global markets and the unwinding can create great volatility as we saw in the 3rd - 4th quarters of 2008. Therefore, if you are entering a carry trade strategy, keep an eye on portfolio drawdown and have a plan for exit.

How can intermarket analysis and cross asset correlations be used effectively when analysing currencies?

Very effectively if you move from general assumptions like "when oil goes up, the US Dollar Index (USDI) goes down" or "if the S&P500 goes down, the USDI goes up." What if those events don't happen? A real simple method of translating movements in and out of correlation between asset classes is simply using a 20-day rate of return cross. In other words, if the USDI has a better return in the last 20 days than the Deutsche Bank Liquid Commodity Index (DBLCI) (regardless of positive or negative return), then a trader can buy the USDI and short when the return is lower. At the same time, pair the prevailing USDI trade the opposite direction with the DBLCI.

Figure 2 represents the USDI trading long/short 100% of the portfolio with no paired trade; the USDI buy and hold; the DBLCI long/short 100% of the portfolio with no USDI paired trade; the DBLCI buy and hold; and the USDI and DBLCI long/short paired trades. Notice the reduction of volatility of the USDI long/short versus the USDI buy and hold with essentially the same end result. Also, notice the large difference of returns by using the USDI as a long/short indicator for DBLCI compared to the DBLCI buy and hold. This is a method of entry point selection with two index streams that tend to inversely correlate. This chart also represents the near top of the DBLCI. To reinforce, a trader needs to be diligent to use protective stops and/or use competing lookback periods if using this strategy.

USING TA IN TRADING

Can you explain your approach to risk and money management?

Our firm treats risk and limitation of drawdown as its primary focus. If declines can be contained to manageable levels, the stress of having to dig out of the hole is substantially reduced. Most traders understand the concept of return stress after a tremendous decline – it takes 100% retracement from a bad trade to breakeven after a 50% decline. Most humans who value a good night's sleep cannot really afford to insert a 50% portfolio decline into their lifestyle because of the limited amount of years to make up that kind of decline.

What impact did the turmoil in 2008 have on your returns? What action have you taken to reduce any losses?

For our currency model, which ultimately became The Currency Strategies Fund (ticker: FOREX), 2008 was turmoil-less. The model had a positive result in 2008, and when management commenced for our private clients in May of 2008, the result was slightly negative at the end of 2008. The success of the model became known amongst advisors and demand picked up. At that point, putting it out in a mutual fund so that advisors could easily use our strategy became a reality for us.

When I built the model in early 2008, I added a "Black Swan Event switch," in other words, a circuit breaker to protect the assets when events that are way beyond the realm of normal expectations occur. These are events of large consequence and can produce a change in history. This entailed a simple exit plan in the face of complexity and to handle the "25 to 50 year" outlier. The circuit breaker was tested about three months after committing client money to the model when the "25 to 50 year" outlier occurred. The detection that something was happening began in the first week of August 2008 when the commodity currencies had an unusual decline and with an increase of almost 50% in the 20 rolling day standard deviation indicator.

The DBLCI had already begun a sharp decline a month earlier. The European currencies were also falling sharply in tandem with the commodity currencies. Even after the level of volatility rose in various currencies, they kept on rising to the point of 300% to 800% the levels had been in July, 2008. Our action was to cross hedge currencies – specifically, the euro, Canadian dollar, British pound, and Japanese yen against the USDI until volatility levels began subsiding (we were also cross hedging equal weighted S&P sectors against the S&P500 cap weighted index in that same period). The results were portfolios that had extremely low volatility throughout the 4th quarter of 2008.

What are the key performance parameters you look at apart from return?

Drawdown is the big one for us, being that we operate as an absolute return business. Win ratio does not mean much in volatile markets because the key is to keep the portfolio decline to a minimum and that requires trading and taking whipsaws in the chin regularly. In rising markets with stable volatility, win ratios are important; that means you are making money.

How do you decide on which position size to take? How much of your capital are you prepared to risk at any one time?

We take position sizes that are equal weighted. We have found through quite a bit of research that equal weighted portfolios strongly outperform cap weight or concentrated bets over rolling 3 year, rolling 5 year, and rolling 10 year periods for the last 20+ years. This is especially true for equities. So, we adhere to an equal weighted methodology within each currency type within the fund.

What level of draw down are you prepared to tolerate?

Realistically, we try to avoid double-digit drawdown in the overall portfolios. The currency portfolio specifically is designed to have low drawdown. We hope to have outlier periods of high single digit drawdown and average drawdowns of less than 5%. Since the fund has been out in May 2009, the maximum drawdown has been -2.8%.

How do measure the degree of risk associated with each trade you make?

There are a series of stop-loss and re-entry levels assigned to each currency. Roughly 70% of the time we can predict our worst case scenario on a per currency basis if they breach each stop loss-level. Another 25%+ of the time, volatility will cause more trading which can negatively (or positively) affect the anticipated worst case scenario NAV. Finally, about 5% of time volatility is so great that a specific currency is left out until its volatility level subsides. So, the degree of risk is preloaded prior to making a trade, and the equal weighting of currencies spreads the risk out.

Do you use stop losses? How do you decide where to place stops?

Stop orders are trail price movement. Simultaneously, the counter trade many times will give buy signals for re-entry or added allocation. Once the stop order has been breached, we begin trading out of the position to reach the new target allocation. This see-saw effect of trading in and out of opposing positions with shallow trailing stops help smooth out the performance of the fund.

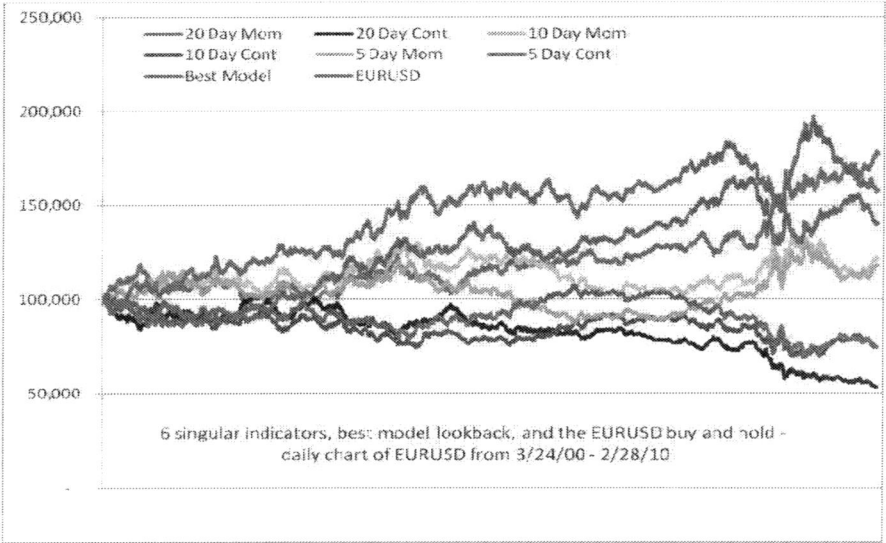

6 singular indicators, best model lookback, and the EURUSD buy and hold - daily chart of EURUSD from 3/24/00 - 2/28/10

Figure 1:

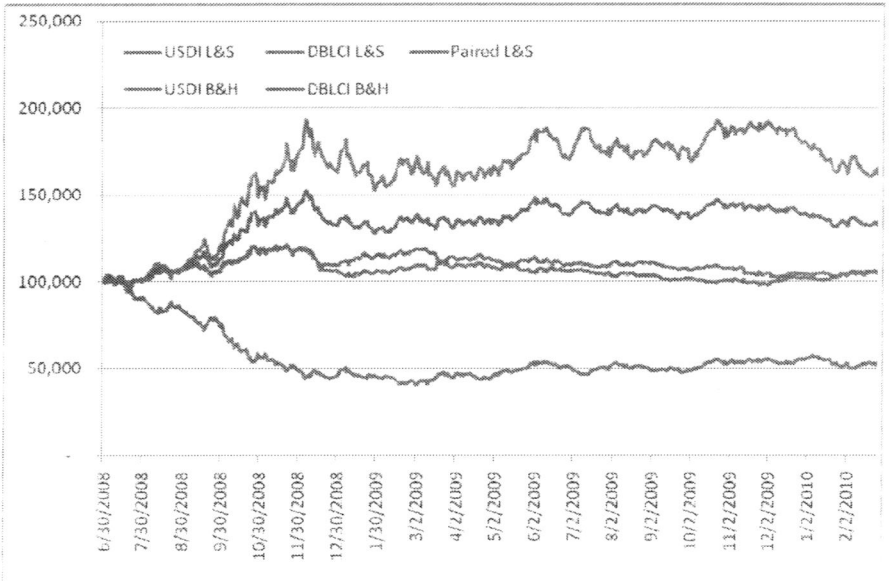

Figure 2:

Chapter 9

WILLIAM O'DONNELL

HEAD US TREASURY STRATEGY

ROYAL BANK OF SCOTLAND

Bill O'Donnell recently re-joined RBS in New York after a four year spell at UBS where he was head of US rates strategy. Before that he spent 20 years as an analyst with Greenwich Capital. He is the primary author of RBS's popular 'Morning Call' research note to clients.

USING TA FOR RESEARCH AND TRADING

Can you explain your basic research/trading style?

My basic research style is this: the synthesis of technical and fundamental analysis to develop an outlook for the market. I am convinced that the two sciences are highly complementary and powerful for those tasked to have an outlook every day.

Which markets do you cover?

I cover FX, US treasuries, energy and the commodity markets.

How does your application of TA differ for short, medium and long-term time scales?

Daily charts provide me with trend signals and support and resistance levels within a 1-day to 3-month timeframe. Most of the investors who read my work probably care most about where the markets are heading over the next 1-3 months. The daily chart is routinely the best in assisting me with a view over that horizon. I used to be an active user of hourly charts but I can't keep changing views every few days since I'd drive my core, institutional readership crazy. I do pay close attention to weekly charts and I often check the monthly charts on my market.

I watch the weekly and monthly charts for two reasons: I have to know what the 'prevailing breezes' are in my market. Indeed, the sailing analogy is a good one for this issue of periodicity. I consider my daily charts as a guide to the local market breezes while the weekly and monthly charts offer me clues as to what the prevailing breezes or trends are. I also use weekly and monthly charts to make sure that I am not missing long-term trendlines that might not be obvious in the more truncated window of my daily chart. I also watch for changes in weekly and monthly momentum studies and I always have a keen eye out for candlestick reversal patterns in my long term charts.

Do you think that the FX markets are more technically driven than other markets?

I follow other markets apart from FX but I know this: TA is everywhere. Few in the cash Treasury markets followed technical analysis until the start of financial futures trading in Chicago in 1976. As the financial futures and the cash markets steadily linked up, the technicians on the floor of the Chicago pits began to exert influence on Treasury traders in New York. It was then that investors in the cash bond markets caught on to technical analysis, as their brethren in futures and stocks had for years.

Now almost everyone in the Treasury markets follows charts of some kind. The ubiquity of chart services and data have given TA a truly mass appeal and therefore I'd posit that FX markets are no more technically driven than other large and developed markets.

How 'random' or efficient are the FX markets compared to the equity or fixed income markets?

At times of crisis few markets are really efficient. Within fixed income, some markets are quite inefficient today because they trade discontinuously. The formerly liquid commercial mortgage backed securities market (CMBS) hardly trades in the wake of the recent downturn. I am sure that pockets of the generally efficient FX and Equities markets are sometimes random too. Even so, I consider all three markets as some of the most efficient on earth. When the black box guys are moving servers closer to the exchanges to get a millisecond leg up, you know you've got efficient markets.

To what extent are the FX markets driven by sentiment?

Well, price is as good a sentiment indicator as any. If you think about it, much of what technicians do is to divine sentiment and sentiment trends by watching prices and price trends.

What are the best sentiment indicators to use?

My favorite sentiment indicator is the Daily Sentiment Index (DSI) for futures published by Jake Bernstein at MBH Commodities. I have been a long time subscriber and I consider their sentiment surveys to be an essential arrow in my quiver. They publish a daily survey of % bulls in FX, commodities and financial futures contracts.

I watch the survey on the financials most closely but I do keep an eye out for extremes in other contracts. For example, right now (April 2010) the euro has become a bit of a risk barometer in the wake of the Greek debt crisis. When bullish sentiment on the euro plunged to a low extreme, that signal gave me a sense that risk aversion was widespread and perhaps overdone. The daily DSIs can be quite noisy for my purposes so I use a 5-day moving average of the DSI to highlight sentiment extremes.

I take notice when the 5-day DSIs get to either 15% Bulls or less or 85% Bulls or greater. When the 5-day DSIs get to <10% Bulls or >90% Bulls, then you have an excellent sign that a trend is getting long in the tooth. If such readings appear when your market is testing support/resistance, you see a candlestick reversal, a major trend breaks or when momentum studies are turning, then you've got the makings of a powerful signal.

Are there any market conditions under which TA works better or worse than other times?

It depends on how good the technical analyst is in determining whether we're in a range market or what the veracity of the trend in the market is. I keep hearing that range bound markets chop technicians to ribbons. Well, the problem stems from failing to identify the range and setting the period of your charts and studies appropriately.

In a trending market go long in period and in a rangebound market shorten up your period(s) commensurate with the span of the actual or expected range. To me, this is the essential art of technical analysis. Let's think of a runner for this question. When a runner hits a steep incline, they should typically shorten up their stride. On a downhill, a runner should lift their knees and lengthen their stride as much as possible. The same is true is TA. In a tight range, you have to shorten up the period of the chart and in a trending market you lengthen the period. This is why pattern and trend analysis is essential to TA; they help to set the appropriate chart period for the conditions.

INDICATORS AND STRATEGIES

Are there any indicators that work especially well in the FX markets?

I am a huge fan and follower of slow stochastics. They are what I grew up on and I've learned their idiosyncrasies along the way. I also use candlestick patterns to help me identify trend reversals.

Which candlestick patterns are most effective?

One of the most reliable reversal patterns in candlesticks is the Morning and Evening Star formation. One is the opposite of the other and the Evening Star comes at the top of price move. Morning Stars show their mettle at market lows. The Evening Star is roughly defined as a 3-period event where there is a sharp upward move in period 1 followed by a gap to new highs in period 2. This is followed by a sharp move lower where the price action of period 3 retraces into the real body of period 1.

The Evening Doji Star is a rarer and more ominous version of the Evening Star and its characteristic comes from period 2 where the close and the open are the same (a Doji in candlestick parlance). This formation is akin to an Island Reversal but with a Doji in the middle. The significance of the Doji is that the matching opening and closing levels signals a new balance of buyers and sellers at the extremes of a trend. Trends are driven by a supply and demand *imbalance* of course. A good example of an Evening Doji Star is shown in Figure 1. I have highlighted the 3-day pattern and you can see how well it worked.

Another reversal pattern that I watch is the Hammer pattern. It's not a reversal pattern per se, but it's a fair warning of an impending trend change in the market. A Hammer Bottom is when the open and close relationship (know as the real body) in a session lie near the top of the period's range. The Hammer Top or Inverted Hammer is just the opposite; the real body is observed at the bottom of a period's range where new range highs were touched during that period. This pattern is pretty common as I show in the time series of daily 10yr Treasury yields (Figure 2). The Hammer is a sign that investors have begun to lean against a trend and may be gaining the upper hand. I have often observed that the end of the trend is defined by a Hammer pattern.

What is your reaction when the charts show a very obvious technical pattern such as a head-and-shoulders or a double top?

I have never been a fan of deriving signals from double tops or head-and-shoulders patterns. They have failed me more than they've worked.

How do you indentify when a trend has commenced and may be nearing its end?

Slow stochastics (14/3 are the periods I use) is my personal favorite though the 9-bar RSI and the ADX are also excellent price momentum tools. There is another excellent indicator for markets that have so little momentum that they can be deemed coiled and trend-ready (especially important information for options traders): the Trend Intensity indicator published daily by IFR Markets. They don't cover many commodities but it's an excellent indicator for highlighting markets devoid of thrust and ready to move.

What is the best method for measuring price momentum in the market?

I am not a fan of Fibonacci numbers (I always find analysts choose the right Fib number after the trend has expired). I do use a simple version of Elliott Wave when I see flags or pennants to get measured moves (as in A=C). I have never used Gann techniques but know some very successful traders who have.

How do you use moving averages? If so, which periodicities do you use and do you use them directly to generate trade signals?

I do not use moving averages. I have a good friend in the business, Jim Chorek of UBS, who is an excellent technician who plies his trade in cycle studies in FX. He proved to me that moving averages, or moving average pairs, should really change constantly to mirror the rhythm of the markets at the time. I hear that and I assume it's easier for me to click between daily, weekly and monthly charts to get an overall feel for the market. I am sure that many younger than me have already retired after a career of following MAs. I was not schooled in them and I found too many exceptions along the way.

If prices reach a major support level do you wait until it has broken through before buying or selling? If so, by how much?
When prices get to a major support I look at the state of momentum indicators first. Then I will want to see oversold momentum indicators before assuming that supports will hold. What would I look for to confirm a sustained breach of support? I would normally wait for a weekly 3pm close on a Friday to confirm a breakout. I've seen breakouts occur in quiet markets where large traders raid stops set behind a major support level. The bigger and more obvious the support/resistance level the greater the risk that a crowd of stops lays behind that level. Waiting for a Friday 3pm close reduces the risk of getting "hooked" at absolutely the worst location.

How do you judge if a market is overbought or oversold?
My two favorite momentum indicators are the slow stochastic and the 9-bar relative strength index (RSI). I use daily momentum studies for range bound markets and then weekly momentum studies in trending markets. Readings near 80 hint at overbought conditions while readings below 20 indicate oversold conditions.

I get most excited about these readings when extreme readings in the daily and the weekly studies are observed simultaneously. For example, I'd hesitate to deem a market oversold if the daily slow stochastic has fallen to 20 when the weekly slow stochastic is trending down but still in the 50s and mid-range. The mix is important; there are no absolutes as George Lane (father of the stochastic indicator) long cautioned.

I do know technicians who follow MACD and DeMark analysis who are incredibly good at identifying over-extended conditions and market turning points. I have doggedly stuck with what I learned and what has worked for me in the past. A great fear of mine is that watching too many indicators will only increase the "fog of war" while risking paralysis of analysis. Simple is good when it comes to technical analysis.

Can you give an example of how you use the RSI?

In Figure 3 I used the daily RSI in conjunction with simple trend analysis to confirm the breakdown in EUR/USD in late 2009. What the RSI did here is to confirm bearish divergence; a very powerful signal that a bull trend was ripe for reversal. Form September 2009 into early December 2009, the Euro was making higher highs against the USD while the RSI (lower panel) was making lower highs. This suggested that the rally in the Euro was getting technically weaker and subject to complete collapse.

How far out do you analyze the FX markets? What specific strategies do you use for longer-term analysis?

My wheelhouse is typically 1-3 months and I rely on my daily charts for most of those calls (watching weekly and monthly charts in the background). When I see weekly momentum change or long term trends break, I will give outlooks that are typically around 6-months in duration. At rare times I will make multi-year calls when really long term trends break and/or momentum turns in my monthly charts.

To what extent do you look at fundamental information?

My experience has taught me that fundamentals drive trends but technicals are better than fundamentals at sniffing out turning points in those trends. I care a lot about fundamentals and I think every technician should. Analysts need to know when releases are coming out and how the market may be leaning for the outcome.

Consider also the beginnings of the so-called Great Recession in 2008. My economics training helped me greatly in understanding the critical link between the housing market and the broader US economy. Other relatively simple observations made clear that the US financial system and US households were highly leveraged and interconnected, with housing at the center of it all. This told me that the risk of recession was high and that rates were too high. I therefore ignored the persistent overbought signals from the shorter term daily studies as rates began their plunge. I instead focused on the longer-term indicators to keep me in a game that was likely to be a long and drawn out affair. My work in fundamental analysis was key to allowing me to stay with a big trade.

How do you combine the application of TA and fundamentals in your analysis?

Work tirelessly, watch everything and speak to experts you trust in other disciplines. I write more about market technicals than I do about fundamentals. Even so, I spend the lion's share of my day reviewing and discussing the ever-changing fundamental picture. My holy grail is to find that critical moment when the technicals and the fundamentals line up. This is the genesis of a great market call. For me, such a time came in the middle of 2007 when rates were still high and oversold, the housing markets were clearly falling, and credit conditions were rapidly deteriorating. The outcome became clear thanks to work done in both technicals and fundamentals.

What determines 'key levels' in the FX markets?

Key levels are derived from previous congestions points or former range boundaries, previous highs and lows set after longer-term moves, and long-term trendlines.

Do you keep an eye on volume levels and if so, how do you use them in your decisions? What is the best source of volume data for the FX markets?

I do watch volume in conjunction with major trend breaks. In my market we can watch futures volume and I also have developed means to measure all trading volumes in our inter-dealer broker screens. I am sure others have done the same on the numerous FX trading platforms. I always like to see a volume surge during a trend break. It helps to confirm that the break is real.

How do you deal with false signals?

They are the unfortunate bane of our business. Indeed, I've long thought that being 60% right in my calls would make me one of the top Wall Street analysts. I think you can achieve this high standard by marrying TA with fundamental analysis. When I do get a false signal, my stop will be triggered and I stop myself out. I then decompose the trade to see where I went wrong. I never forget the false signals and that helps to shape your experience to avoid the pitfalls of false signals in the future. Nothing is more important in TA than experience.

Figure 1: A Doji Evening Star   Source: CQG

Figure 2: Hammer Bottoms and Top   Source: CQG

Figure 3: RSI bearish divergence   Source: CQG

Chapter 10

SHAUN OSBORNE

CHIEF FX STRATEGIST

TD SECURITIES

Shaun Osborne is TD Securities' Chief FX Strategist based in Toronto where he writes daily and weekly analytical reports on the foreign exchange markets. Before this he worked as an analyst for Thomson/IFR and Informa Global Markets in London and Paris.

USING TA FOR RESEARCH AND TRADING

Can you explain your basic research/trading style?

I take a very straightforward approach with technical analysis. I only use candlestick charts and very few oscillators or moving average signals. I like candlestick charts because I think they give a very immediate sense of what is going on in the market. The reversal and continuation signals that candlesticks convey are relatively simple to understand and appreciate. Providing the data source is reliable, I find candlesticks give generally reliable signals.

However, I do use one oscillator consistently, which is the Direction Movement Index (DMI). The DMI is a useful signal for assessing the underlying trend strength in markets. For currency markets, I particularly look for alignment of price signals or momentum trends over multiple timeframes. When the DMI signal is suggesting a strongly trending bull or bear market over the hourly, daily and weekly timeframes, I can be very confident that the market is going to move consistently in the direction of the underlying trend. More often than not, these situations also produce fairly rapid market moves which see relatively minor, or no, counter-trend corrections.

Which markets do you cover?

I am principally responsible for the technical coverage of the majors, or G7/10 currencies. Working for a Canadian bank, I spend a lot of

148

my day looking at the Canadian dollar. That means not just the CAD versus the USD or Euro or Japanese yen but also markets that could have an impact on the CAD's performance, such as crude oil or other commodities.

How does your application of TA differ for short, medium and long-term time scales?

I use the same techniques over multiple time frames. For example, when I look at USD/CAD, I have a 1-hour, 6-hour, daily and weekly candle chart all set up on the same page of my system. I take a top, down approach using the longer-term charts as the basis for my assessment of the overall trend and directional risks. I then use the shorter-term time frames for the intraday trading analysis and trading recommendations. I look to fine-tune support and resistance levels on the shorter-term charts for intraday trading and the longer-term charts for support and resistance zones.

Do you think that the FX markets are more technically driven than other markets?

Not necessarily. I think that technical analysis is simply another way of looking at supply and demand. It looks to identify where there are likely to be buyers and sellers and at what point the longs or the shorts will have to bail out of their positions when the market is moving against them.

How random or efficient are the FX markets compared to the equity or fixed income markets?

Market efficiency is still an issue that is widely debated in academic research. No market can really be entirely efficient otherwise there would be little or no motivation for most investors, or at least those looking for superior returns, to get involved. It seems that the currency market is neither efficient nor entirely random. The research suggests that relatively simple momentum or carry trade strategies can lead to significant profits in the currency market over time and that to some degree technical trading rules do provide some added value in trying to beat the market.

To what extent are the FX markets driven by sentiment? Is this possible to quantify?

Sentiment is very difficult to quantify in my opinion. Given that the foreign exchange market is an un-regulated, largely OTC market with no centralised clearing system for trades, we get very little timely information on volume or flows. Banks have therefore developed their own studies of client flows and trend to try and gain some insight into investor sentiment but, by definition, this can only represent a small snapshot of the entire market.

What are the best sentiment indicators to use?

Given the paucity of reliable sentiment indicators, data provided by the CFTC on positioning in IMM-traded currency contracts (COT report) is perhaps the only sentiment indicator that provides any significant insight. But there are some clear drawbacks even with this data. The data are released with something of a lag (Friday afternoon, covering the trading week through to the prior Tuesday) and represent a relatively small part of the overall currency market flow. As a basic indicator of bullish, bearish or changing market sentiment, this is one series that I do pay some attention to.

Does the application of TA differ when using it to analyse a currency index as compared to currency pairs?

Few currency indices are published with the depth of data that would be required for solid technical analysis; most central bank currency indices comprise end-of-day only data, for example. Comparable currency indices (the Bank of England publishes data for a wide range of currencies) can provide the basis for relative value analysis as these data (re-indexed to the same level and using the same starting point) illustrate clearly the relative under- or out-performance of currencies over time.

The NYBOT DXY Index is a widely followed index measuring the US dollar's performance against six major currencies. The index is heavily weighted towards the Euro, which comprises a little more than 57% of the basket and generally tends to reflect the US dollar's performance against the single currency as a result.

Are there any market conditions under which TA works better or worse than other times?

Illiquid and volatile market conditions, when fear and panic take over as the primary motivators of investor behaviour, typically lead to conditions where technical signals command little or no respect.

INDICATORS AND STRATEGIES

What is your reaction when the charts show a very obvious technical pattern such as a head-and-shoulders or a double top?

I like to look at the formation in the context of the overall market to try and figure out if what the signal is telling me fits with what might be expected at that particular stage in the markets. A significant reversal signal after an extended move might be a little more important as a signal than a double top in a market that appears to be moving sideways or range trading, for example.

How do you indentify when a trend has commenced and may be nearing its end?

A well-defined trend is rarely obvious until the move is well developed. As a first step, look for consistently rising (higher highs) or falling prices (lower lows). Drawing a simple parallel channel with at least four points of reference (two support and two resistance) helps define the potential for the trend to develop. Moving outside of that basic trend can highlight an accelerating trend (if price starts to fall more quickly) or a decelerating trend (if the trend starts to flatten out).

What is the best method for measuring price momentum in the market?

The only oscillator study I use every day is the Directional Movement Index (DMI) as I think this study provides the best assessment of trend momentum. Figure 1 shows the DMI being used for EURUSD from 2008-09.

Do you use Fibonacci, Gann or Elliott Wave techniques and if so, how?

Once I think I have identified a turn in the market after a lengthy move in one direction, I will use Fibonacci techniques to try and assess the scope for a retracement in the market (Figure 2). I have never used Gann or Elliott Wave.

Do you use moving averages? If so, which periodicities do you use and do you use them directly to generate trade signals?

As gauges of short, medium or long-term support and resistance, the basic moving average signals are hard to ignore if only because the market knows that everyone else is also paying attention to the 11, 21, 55 or 200-day moving averages. Some markets seem to be a little more sensitive to some tenors than others and some optimization work may be required to try and find the moving average (or pair of averages) that works best in the market you are trying to analyse.

If prices reach a major support level do you wait until it has broken through before buying or selling? If so, by how much?

This boils down to a judgement call for most people. For signals on short-term charts, I like to see prices break support by at least 5-10 ticks. Regardless of the time-frame though, I prefer to see the break hold through the close of the hour, day or week, depending on the time frame of the chart that I am using, to underpin the potential for a real break out.

How do you judge if a market is overbought or oversold?

Oscillator studies can provide some help here but the RSI or slow stochastic studies can only go so far in indicating that a market is in an overbought or oversold state. That does not mean the trend is going to turn any time soon. I rely less on oscillator signals these days than earlier in my technical analyst career because I have been often frightened away from a market that has continued to trend even when the oscillator signal has been signalling overbought or oversold.

I prefer to pay close attention to the price action. If the trend is starting to flatten out or if the market is still rising (or falling) in a narrowing range (forming a descending or ascending wedge, in other words), the move may be running out of steam.

CHARACTERISTICS UNIQUE TO THE FX MARKETS

What intraday effects impact the FX markets?

Daily fixings or month-end flows as asset managers adjust their foreign currency hedges or rebalance their positions according to their benchmarks can sometimes produce significant flows. Whether these flows have a major impact on the markets can depend on volumes and liquidity in the market at the time.

How far out do you analyse the FX markets? What specific strategies do you use for longer-term analysis?

I tend to concentrate on a 3-6 month window for longer-term technical calls. I use the same basic techniques for analysing the longer-term trends in the market as I do for analysing the short-term trends.

Is there any difference in your approach between the analysis of G7 and emerging markets currencies? To what extent is liquidity in EM markets a factor?

My main focus is on the G-7/10 currencies and their respective cross rates so I tend to spend less time looking at emerging markets. Given that most developing market currencies are somewhat less liquid or trade relatively thinly outside of their own time zones, some caution is warranted when dealing with short-term signals. I tend to confine my analysis of these markets to broader assessments of market trends and risks rather than finely tuned intraday analysis.

To what extent do you look at fundamental information?

I follow fundamental developments very closely. I think most market participants follow both technical and fundamental developments. Fundamental analysis provides the cornerstones for currency analysis and technical signals provide entry and exit points for positioning and, perhaps most importantly from a risk-management point of view, where to get out of a trade if it is going against you.

What fundamental information is most important for the FX markets?

For the US economy example, in the 1980s, money supply data was the main monthly focus for the markets because the Fed was battling to control inflation. Then in the 1990s it was the monthly trade data due to the worries about the US twin deficits. More recently, the non-farm payroll report has become the primary focus for the markets.

What is the best method of measuring volatility in the FX markets?

Most analytical systems will provide a tool to measure volatility in any market. Fore currency traders, typical volatility measures would look at 10-day or 30-day volatility.

Are there any specific currency pairs that are more prone to trending?

Low volatility, widening interest rate spreads and low returns in other markets all combined to provide the ideal conditions to drive carry trades in the currency markets between 2004 and 2008. This produced an almost relentless rise in higher yielding currencies, such as the Euro and Australian dollar versus the low-yielding Japanese yen. Once market volatility started to increase – rapidly in 2007 and 2008 and global interest rates began to decline again as the credit crunch started to bite – the conditions were ideal for a massive liquidation trade.

What determines the 'key levels' in the FX markets?

Major highs and lows, or where major highs and lows have converged, are a prime example of what FX traders would consider to be important levels. The longer-term moving averages, such as the 55-day or 200-day, also command respect in the markets. Key levels can also be significant round numbers for specific currency pairs. For example, the pound first traded under $2.00 to the USD in 1947 and did not get back to that point until the 1980s. Since then, the pound has been able to sustain gains above $2.00 on relatively rare occasions. Similarly, the Canadian dollar's move above parity to the US dollar in 2007 was widely anticipated before the event actually occurred in November of that year. Despite enormous pressure on the US dollar, a break through par was not easy to achieve. These levels could be termed psychologically key levels for the market.

To what extent are FX markets seasonal? Can you give some examples of seasonality in the currency markets?

Seasonal factors can have some influence on currency markets but I generally think the overall impact is relatively small and not entirely consistent. One example would be the expectation that repatriation of overseas investments back to Japan running into the Japanese fiscal year end on March 31st boosts the Japanese yen. There is not a consistent trend towards notable yen appreciation in March, in my opinion, but there is perhaps a little more volatility in the exchange rate around that time. Whether that is caused by repatriation or the expectation of repatriation in the markets (or a combination of both) is hard to quantify.

How do you measure the impact that fund flows have on specific currencies?

Most official flow of funds data is released with a lag. These numbers are often useful for indicating which asset class investors are favouring over time and where the investment is coming from but most banks also try and assess their own client flows to gain a more dynamic insight into currency trends.

Is it true that currencies are especially susceptible to market rumours? If so, why is this?

Market rumours are certainly present in the foreign exchange market although I am not sure that the FX market is any more susceptible to rumours than others.

Is the carry trade still applicable for some currency pairs?

The carry trade has been a reliable generator of excess return for investors in recent years and remains a valid strategy for market investors. At the end of 2009, the FX analysis team at TD Securities thought that the time was ripe for re-establishing a carry trade strategy based on shorting the three lowest yielding G10 currencies (we assessed that the Japanese yen, the British pound and US dollar would likely be the lowest yielding major currencies over the course of the year) while going long the three highest yielding major currencies. We liked the idea of the carry trade because the global investment environment was becoming less volatile and interest rate spreads were widening modestly in favour of the higher yielding currencies. Low volatility and widening interest rate differentials meant that risk-adjusted carry trade returns – an important consideration for asset managers – was improving. The broader environment suited the carry trade, in other words.

The strategy has generated positive returns so far this year but there have been some large swings in returns as the global investment environment remains somewhat volatile and susceptible to setbacks (such as Europe's sovereign credit crisis). The carry trade is still applicable but conditions have to be supportive and investors have to manage risk constantly.

How is the impact on FX rates of the carry trade best measured?

According to economic theory, the carry trade should not work. The benefit derived from higher interest rates should be offset by the higher yielding currency's depreciation over time. This, of course, is not always the case but we should not completely disregard the theory.

An example of this is the Australian dollar/Japanese yen carry trade, which was popular for investors between 2001 and 2007. At the time, Australian interest rates were rising steadily while Japanese interest rates were locked near zero, volatility was close to historic lows, and liquidity was abundant. The cross rose steadily from JPY56 to a peak of JPY107 in 2007; a return of over 90% in addition to the yield derived from holding Australian dollars. When the credit crunch started to inject more volatility into markets and raise the prospect that interest rates around the world would have to fall, the Australian dollar collapsed. In the space of three months in 2008, it fell from JPY104.50 all the way back to 56. A 46% fall that unwound all the appreciation in the cross rate in the prior seven years.

This is an example of a popular trade that had just become too crowded. When everyone wanted to get out at the same time, the result was financial market carnage; the liquidation of carry trades probably contributed significantly to the financial market volatility that developed over the course of 2007 and 2008. The carry trade is a reliable strategy if supportive conditions prevail, but investors have to remember that higher rewards usually entail higher risk and that risk has to be managed appropriately.

Is it possible to differentiate between times when the market is being driven by speculators and by hedgers?

The vast majority of daily turnover in the FX market is driven by interbank trading, proprietary trading or speculative trading from a range of different agents in the market. This activity is typically more than enough to overwhelm corporate hedging activity.

How can intermarket analysis and cross asset correlations be used effectively when analysing currencies?

Cross-market correlations are useful for analysing broader trends and market inter-relationships but it is important to remember that correlations ebb and flow over time and constant monitoring is required here as well. One recent example is the strong inverse correlation that was evident between equity markets and the USD in 2008 and 2009 (Figure 3). The relationship reflected the risk seeking or risk-averse behaviour in financial markets. If investors were in risk-seeking mode, equities and other riskier assets would rise and the safe-haven US dollar would decline. Alternatively, if investors were concerned by developments in the markets and moved out of riskier assets, the US dollar was a natural, liquid refuge.

The relationship proved durable and particularly persistent through much of the credit crisis and helped frame the broader market condition at the time. From a trading perspective, these sorts of relationships can help with positioning. If an investor was bearish on equities, a natural complement to that position would be a long US dollar position. Equally, this relationship would have indicated that asset managers should avoid having a net long equity and long USD position on their books at the same time as the strong inverse correlation in daily returns meant that they would be almost guaranteed not to make money.

Do you keep an eye on volume levels and if so, how do you use them in your decisions? What is the best source of volume data for the FX markets?

With no central exchange to provide volume data for the foreign exchange market, the only sources for this sort of information are the Chicago futures pits and in-house or proprietary data. The IMM data are a pretty good proxy for the broader market, I think, as they tend to capture rising and falling speculative interest quite well. Generally, I pay attention to big jumps or declines in volumes as this might suggest a change in investor behaviour in response to an event or in anticipation of a new development (such as a change in interest rate policy). Extreme volumes can indicate an over-extended market that is vulnerable to a position squeeze.

Figure 1: Weekly DMI for EURUSD

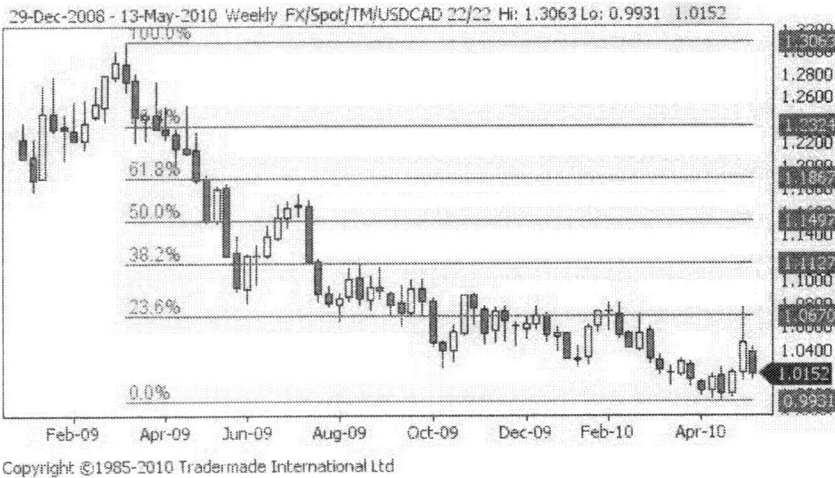

Figure 2: Fibonacci retracements for USDCAD

Figure 3: US dollar index versus S&P500

Chapter 11

KATIE STOCKTON

CHIEF MARKET TECHNICIAN

MKM PARTNERS

Katie Stockton is the chief market technician for MKM Partners, an equity research, sales and trading firm in Connecticut, US. Prior to joining MKM in 2004, she worked as a trader for New York-based hedge fund Ulysses Management and was an analyst for Morgan Stanley's technical strategy group.

USING TA FOR RESEARCH AND TRADING

Can you explain your basic research/trading style?

I am a trading oriented technician with a focus on short and intermediate-term time horizons, which is where TA adds the most value in my opinion. Of course, without a sense of the primary long-term trend, it is nearly impossible to identify short and intermediate-term turning points. To this end, momentum and trend-following indicators are at the forefront of my work. I also make a point to be aware of support and resistance levels and overbought/oversold measures, which are essential for risk management.

In order to stay one step ahead of the market, I am always on the lookout for new indicators or those that are not widely followed. For example, the Rex Oscillator is of interest to me presently. Lesser known tools can give an edge that is immeasurable, and their viability is not as easily chalked up to their self-fulfilling nature. It is also a good exercise to change parameters from time-to-time for the more popular tools, like the MACD indicator and stochastics, to see what is working best.

Which markets do you cover?

The increasingly global nature of the market calls for an understanding of other regions and asset classes. Inter-market relationships are incredibly important, so I am constantly reviewing major commodities, currencies and fixed income. Attitudes toward risk are perhaps captured best by the FX market, which lends itself well to TA. The correlations are always changing, but can be very telling. For example, the trend of the US dollar can give an idea of the direction of the S&P 500, given its inverse relationship to the Dollar Index, which is always on my radar.

Movements in commodities are a reflection of the macroeconomic environment and can also affect stocks, particularly in the basic materials and energy sectors. For this reason, I feature crude oil and gold regularly in my research, in addition to the 10-year Treasury yield which also contributes macroeconomic insight. Interestingly, technical indicators can also be applied to economic data like the unemployment rate, which is a worthwhile endeavour. I have had success applying the monthly TD Sequential™ and TD Combo™ models, created by Tom DeMark, in addition to the MACD indicator.

Why do you think the USD is so closely correlated with the S&P? Has this changed in recent years and if so, why?

In my opinion, the negative correlation between the US dollar and the S&P500 is driven, at least partially, by a concurrent increase in interest rates. The debate is better suited for an economist, but some view a strong currency as an impediment to growth, which drives them to look outside the US for investment opportunities. The correlation between the Dollar Index (DXY), which averages the exchange rates between the US dollar and six major currencies, and the S&P500 fluctuates, but in recent years has been about -40%.
Peaks in the DXY are associated with troughs in the S&P500, and vice versa.

For example, the DXY topped in early 2002 just a few months before the S&P500. More recently, the DXY bottomed in early 2008, just a few months after the S&P500 peaked. From a short-term perspective, a look at the 50-day moving averages of each series reveals that the negative correlation diverged in Q1 2010. Like any intermarket relationship, the DXY/S&P500 comparison needs to be viewed within the context of the current economic environment, and with the knowledge that there will be divergences at times.

How does your application of TA differ for short, medium and long-term time scales?

In theory, the same analysis should apply to all timeframes, but in practice different approaches seem appropriate. The same indicators apply to medium and long-term time horizons with only minor tweaks. For example, a 200-day moving average on a daily bar chart is replaced by a 40-week moving average on a weekly bar chart. This way, the primary trend is revealed without losing the moving average's self-fulfilling property as potential support and resistance.

Intraday timeframes call for more sensitive indicators with parameters that are high-frequency without giving too many signals. Tom DeMark's indicators work particularly well on sub-60 minute bar charts, especially when combined with identification of support and resistance.

Do you think that the FX markets are more technically driven than other markets?

It is not entirely accurate to call any market "technically driven," in my opinion. It is a phrase often used to explain a price move that seems unexplainable on the surface. In reality, there are likely economic or fundamental forces at work that simply are not obvious to everyone. Of course, where there is a lot of uncertainty, usually over short-term time horizons, TA can help fill in the blanks. However, there definitely are situations in which breakouts or breakdowns generate price momentum simply because the chart is widely followed. Trends *can* be self-propelled for a stretch, but it is my belief that the foundation for the moves in the FX markets can generally be explained by fundamental, macroeconomic and/or geopolitical forces.

With that in mind, the FX markets do trend more reliably than most, likely a function of their liquidity and what could be considered a relatively pure supply-and-demand relationship. Headline risk seems less acute for currencies than it is for stocks, in my opinion, and they seem subject to fewer false moves. In turn, changes in trend in the FX markets are often easier to identify.

How 'random' or efficient are the FX markets compared to the equity or fixed income markets?

TA has its foundation in the identification of trends and recurring price patterns, calling into question the randomness of all markets. In

163

general, the behaviour of markets is driven by investor psychology, with the battle between supply and demand a reflection of their belief in the ability of a company or government to deliver on its promises. With this in mind, the FX markets should be equal to the equity and fixed income markets in terms of their randomness. However, as noted, the FX markets tend to provide a clearer reflection of supply and demand, and tend to trend more reliably, in my experience.

To what extent are the FX markets driven by sentiment? Is this possible to quantify?

In a sense, 100% of the move in any market is sentiment-driven, because it reflects investors' perception of all available information, which becomes the source of all buy and sell orders. However, sentiment as it is commonly referred to by technical analysts tends to encompass contrarian measures that are difficult, but not impossible to quantify. The investor polls are laborious, but do yield actual percentages of bulls and bears and transactional sentiment indicators provide an objective view of how investors are positioning. At extremes, sentiment indicators can confirm or contradict trends in price, although at other times they may be simply anecdotal.

Does the application of TA differ when using it to analyse a currency index as compared to currency pairs?

The same charts can be used to analyse currency indices and currency pairs. I have found the same indicators apply equally well to most markets and provide a valuable comparison when used across different timeframes. It is a good idea to have some of your computer's real estate dedicated to a view that consists of at least two different timeframes. For example, a daily bar chart that goes back several months next to a weekly bar chart going back several years for an idea of the intermediate and long-term trends and outlooks. Depending on your resources, you may be limited in your ability to apply indicators to pairs, although most can be viewed using a Bloomberg terminal without any issues. Naturally, analysis of thinly traded currency pairs will often be less reliable than currency indices.

Are there any market conditions under which TA works better or worse than other times?

TA is in the eye of the beholder, so to say it works better in a particular environment is misleading. In my experience, it adds value in trend-following and range-bound markets, and human error is the reason it sometimes seems to fail. There are indicators that lend themselves to every environment, and we face the constant challenge of knowing what to give more weight.

Charts occasionally let us down when a positive or negative headline generates a surge in volatility, usually generating a gap above or below an important level(s). Volatility can impair the effectiveness of TA, as it does quantitative and fundamental analysis. For this reason, it is important to be aware of the typical headline risk associated with the instrument in question, in addition to its liquidity. An illiquid market tends to be gappy. Fortunately, TA is a great risk management tool if applied objectively, no matter what conditions the markets bring.

INDICATORS AND STRATEGIES

Are there any indicators that work especially well in the FX markets?

The Japanese cloud model, know as Ichimoku works particularly well for the FX markets, given its global following and its propensity toward steady, well-defined trends. Cloud charts consist of several components, but the one I find most helpful is the cloud itself, a shaded area that is derived from mid-points of price over specified periods (which, not accidentally, are similar to the standard periods for the MACD indicator). The cloud has a forward-looking shift of 26 periods and is best used as a gauge of support and resistance. It also gives a sense of the dominant trend and, like many trend-following indicators, loses its edge in sideways markets.

As of March 2010 I am watching the Dollar Index as it approaches an important cloud resistance level based on the cloud model on a monthly chart (Figure 1), a breakout above which would signal a multi-year shift. Beyond the cloud model, I find other indicators like the MACD indicator and the stochastics to be equally reliable for all markets including FX.

What is your reaction when the charts show a very obvious technical pattern such as a head-and-shoulders or a double top?

Price patterns can reveal themes in the marketplace and should not be ignored. When a certain price pattern is prevalent, my reaction is to inform clients immediately to help them manage risk, whether or not the pattern is completed. Patterns that can be described as "textbook" do not arise often, but when they do the implications can be significant. The double top and head-and-shoulders formations are perfect examples as they yield impressive downside targets after a breakdown (below support) occurs. These patterns are a reflection of market psychology, so when they arise they can be telling and shape my top-down call.

How do you identify when a trend has commenced and may be nearing its end?

In my opinion, the primary goal of TA is to identify when a trend is nearing its end. It is usually fairly easy to identify the current trend, but it is difficult to measure the maturity of that trend *before* a breakout or breakdown has occurred. No one indicator has the answer, but a combination of indicators can be incredibly helpful.

Divergences can give a *feel* for the maturity of a trend, but I look elsewhere to assist in discovering actual inflection points. The DeMark indicators have been the most practical, particularly when applied across more than one timeframe, because of their ability to take most of the subjectivity out of my analysis. My preferred models are TD Sequential™ and TD Combo™, which are the foundation of many of the DeMark indicators, used in conjunction with the 12-3-3 stochastics. This combination can help identify trend exhaustion and generate buy or sell signals in real time.

Of course, trends are more likely to end near important support and resistance levels, so it is essential to have an idea of price levels where there may be buying or selling pressure. This can be achieved by drawing trendlines, using the cloud model, or by identifying Fibonacci levels and historical (but not outdated) peaks and troughs. Knowing which of these support or resistance levels is most important is the art of TA and something we will all spend a career doing.

What is the best method for measuring price momentum in the market?

The MACD indicator is a fantastic tool for identifying important price swings (Figure 2). The common parameters (13, 26 and 9 period moving averages) can give signals that are too frequent on a daily bar chart, so I have begun to use 21, 100 and 200 period moving averages to capture more important intermediate-term shifts. The TMAP model, created by Rick Bensignor, is another helpful indicator of momentum and consists of the 20, 35 and 50 period moving averages, with a yellow light being flashed when the 20 period flattens and a red light when the 50 period is penetrated.

Finally, I have begun to apply the Rex Oscillator developed by Eduardo Moreira in my work with great success. It is a lesser-known tool that gauges where the close is relative to the open, high and low, with the presumption that a close near the high and well above the open is bullish, and vice versa.

Of course, momentum indicators tend to be lagging in nature and therefore are best applied with an overlay of overbought/oversold measures. Their lagging characteristics come from the fact that most are created using moving averages of historical prices and can signal a shift several price bars after the actual pivot point. Using our preferred weekly bar chart, this can mean a lag time of more than a month, creating a situation in which we need to supplement moving average-based models with overbought/oversold measures, most often the DeMark™ indicators.

Do you use Fibonacci, Gann or Elliott Wave techniques and if so, how?

The three techniques are all valid, but I use only the Fibonacci sequence in my research. Gann and Elliott Wave analysis can be quite subjective. The concepts are grounded in sound theory, but in practice I have found the angles and waves become obvious only in hindsight. Fibonacci levels are more obvious to me in real-time. The Fibonacci sequence is fascinating, given its application far beyond the financial markets in things such as nature (i.e., the spacing of tree branches).

The Fibonacci ratios I pay most attention to are 38.2% and 61.8%, which are particularly valuable as support and resistance when viewed as retracements, and can be helpful for deriving price targets when viewed as extensions (Figure 3). It is amazing how markets seem to gravitate toward these levels, as if driven by some magnetic force.

167

Once a 38.2% retracement is exceeded to the upside or downside, it seems that a 61.8% retracement is almost inevitable over the intermediate term. As with most tools, Fibonacci levels are evaluated with a level of subjectivity, stemming primarily from the identification of important highs/lows from which to draw them.

Can you give a short description of the Rex Oscillator?

The Rex Oscillator measures a price bar's close relative to its open, high and low. It is best described as a momentum indicator and it built on the premise that a 'strong' close reflects positive momentum, whereas a 'weak' close reflects negative momentum. The Rex Oscillator is commonly created using a moving average of the "true value of a bar," which is equal to 3 * Close − (Low + Open + High). When the indicator is at a positive divergence with price, it suggests momentum is improving, and when it crosses above zero, it suggests momentum is positive.

What settings do you use for the stochastic?

I use unusual parameters for the stochastic oscillator, described as 12-3-3. This means the calculation uses 12 periods, smoothed by a 3-period moving average (a slow stochastic), with a 3-period moving average used to generate crossovers for signals. These parameters give a desirable frequency of signals, in my opinion. A buy signal occurs when the signal line crosses above the slow stochastic from below the oversold extreme of 20%. A sell signal occurs when the signal line crosses below the slow stochastic from above the overbought extreme of 80%.

One nuance of the indicator, dubbed a 'stochastic pop', is a signature setup of mine. It occurs when the slow stochastic falls from overbought extremes, but quickly recovers and gives way to a crossover and return above 80%. This setup usually reflects strong positive momentum and can be viewed as a buy signal, even when it occurs near overbought extremes.

How do you use moving averages? If so, which periodicities do you use and do you use them directly to generate trade signals?

Moving averages are my primary tool for identifying trends. The 200-day (or 40-week) moving average gives a good sense of the long-term trend (Figure 4), whereas the 50-day (or 10-week) moving average gives a good sense of the intermediate-term trend. Crossovers in these two moving averages simply enhance a reversal in the dominant trend that has become obvious in most cases. Moving averages are lagging by nature, so they will never be adept at identifying turning points. However, in a trending market moving averages can be invaluable for eliminating the short-term "noise" that often is so easy to get caught up in.

Another collection of moving averages that bears watching is the 20, 35 and 50 period moving averages, usually applied to daily and weekly bar charts, described earlier as the TMAP model. This model not only helps identify strong trends, but also provides a trading strategy when momentum appears to be waning. For example, when the 20-period moving average flattens, it suggests one-half of a position should be added or taken off. When the 50-period moving average is penetrated, it suggests a reversal has occurred and that positions should be closed, and in some cases initiated in the other direction. In summary, moving averages are used to create most momentum indicators, including the MACD indicator and Rex Oscillator, and therefore are essential tools for TA.

If prices reach a major support level do you wait until it has broken through before buying or selling? If so, by how much?

Support and resistance represent areas of potential buying and selling pressure, so when they are approached, a reversal in trend can be anticipated. When these levels are broken decisively - meaning two consecutive closes below or above them, there is often a role reversal where support becomes resistance and vice versa. If a support (or resistance) level is broken, in general it gives the chart a lower (or higher) bias, if it was not already previously established. It is not always a sell (or buy) signal, however, given other technical factors that come into play. When I see a breakdown below support, I ask myself the following questions:

- Is the breakdown decisive, meaning consecutive weak closes (more than a penny or two) below the level in question?

- Is the breakdown accompanied by heavy volume?

- Where is secondary support for a gauge of additional risk?

- What is the dominant trend and does it still have momentum?

- Are oversold conditions signalling a recovery rally for a better selling opportunity?

- Is there a counter-trend signal (e.g., a crossover in the stochastics)?

The answers to these questions help us determine whether the breakdown is actionable. It may be better to sell immediately or stay on the sidelines to preserve capital for more exciting opportunities from a technical standpoint. To have paid attention to breakdowns below support would have minimized the damage to many portfolios during the sharp decline in the US equity market in late 2008.

How do you judge if a market is overbought or oversold?

The words overbought/oversold are grossly overused outside the world of TA, so it is important for everyone to understand that these are quantifiable measures with good track records for identifying price swings. If I had to take one overbought/oversold measure to a deserted island, it would be DeMark's TD Sequential™ model. This model runs counts of price that attempt to identify trend exhaustion by comparing the current price bar's high, low or close to a previous bar's open, high, low or close. Some argue that these signals work because they are self-fulfilling. That may be true in some markets, and across some timeframes. However, they also work when applied to obscure currency crosses and futures contracts, which is a challenge to the self-fulfilling nature as being their sole benefit. In my daily scans, I use both the TD Sequential™ and TD Combo™ models.

The stochastic oscillator is another tool that serves the purpose of identifying when buyers or sellers are saturated. Some use the RSI in its place and probably have a similar success rate with it. The stochastics give clear signals via crossovers above 80% (overbought) or below 20% (oversold) to be viewed within the context of momentum. It is one of my favourite tools for finding short opportunities, especially when combined with a momentum overlay, and I use it as a measure of market breadth by tallying overbought/oversold readings among the components of a universe and recording them as a running percentage of the total. Visually, the stochastics are great for determining the importance of interim peaks and troughs and, in this way, can assist in drawing accurate trendlines.

How do you combine the application of TA and fundamentals in your analysis?

Combining disciplines is the key to success in any market. For investing, fundamental analysis and macroeconomic research are often best used to answer "what" and "why," whereas TA is best used to answer "when." At my firm, we try to find situations where a company has a macroeconomic story supporting it, such as promising fundamentals, and a chart that appears to be providing an entry point. The primary drawback of using fundamental analysis *without* TA is that the available data are often monthly or quarterly, leaving investors with the need to interpolate over the short-term. I believe charts can fill in the blanks over the short-term, which is particularly important in volatile environments.

Are the currency markets more or less prone to trending than stocks?

Currencies appear to be more prone to trending than stocks, likely a function of their high liquidity and the dynamics of supply and demand. This means that trend following indicators, like the cloud model, work very well in the analysis of the FX market. This also may be a function of their global following. As always, I would be mindful of countertrend signals generated by overbought/oversold measures or sentiment gauges.

USING TA IN TRADING

Can you explain your approach to risk and money management?

As a research analyst on the sell side, I need to apply risk management of a different kind than most money managers. My risk management involves keeping a close watch of which indicators are working in the current environment and which are not. It is difficult to ascertain in real-time, so I work under the assumption that the market is full of surprises. I am always willing to tweak parameters and shift emphasis among various indicators. For my clients, risk management calls for a respect of support and resistance levels and price trends, of which the indicators are only a derivative. This is a lesson that is often revisited during bear markets, reminding us to go back to the basics of why TA works.

How do you measure the degree of risk associated with each trade you make?

With each recommendation I make the degree of risk can be measured using the proximity of support (or resistance for short recommendations). Support can be derived by previous peaks or troughs on the chart, a moving average, a Fibonacci level, the cloud model, and so on. A stop-loss point can be placed below a support level to minimize downside risk, allowing a disciplined approach to trading.

Which trade exit and entry strategies do you use?

Entry and exit strategies vary in different market environments, but tend to involve a combination of support and resistance in conjunction with overbought/oversold measures. In a strongly trending environment, pullbacks or corrections provide the lowest-risk entries. In an uptrend, pullbacks tend to occur when overbought conditions become widespread among the market's constituents. Knowing when this occurs can help time exits as well.

The ideal entry point for long positions is once overbought conditions are relieved, generating oversold or neutral readings in the stochastics (or a similar measure) near an important support level. I rarely buy something that has been overbought for a prolonged period, unless it has broken out. However, I have no trouble buying something that is newly overbought with bullish momentum characteristics. Momentum can be a complementary indicator for timing entries and exits, and in my opinion is best gauged using signals from the MACD indicator and/or Rex Oscillator. Naturally, positive readings or positive divergences in our momentum indicators lead us to be more aggressive with entries and more conservative with exits, and vice versa.

How do you deal with false signals?

I manage the potential for false signals by waiting for confirmation of breakouts and breakdowns. For confirmation, I require consecutive closes above or below a level, with more weight given to strong closes that are near the high or low of the price bar for the period in question. This helps minimize whipsaws, although it is not perfect. When a false signal materializes in hindsight, it can be very telling. I once heard a quote that went something like, "There's nothing worse than a false breakout," which I believe can be attributed to the late Mike Epstein, and I feel there is some truth to that. If a resistance level is exceeded, meaning that selling pressure is cleared, and there is a lack of upside follow-through, it may reflect something structurally wrong that is not yet widely known. In these cases, I would stay on the sidelines and let the market sort itself out over a period of time. It also is a good habit to check the level of short interest, when possible, as it can sometimes explain moves that have no staying power.

Do you use stop-losses? If so, how do you decide where to place them?

I recommend using support and resistance, as opposed to percentages, as guidelines for where to place stop-losses. In my opinion, a stop-loss is best placed below support for long positions and above resistance for short positions. I recommend waiting for consecutive daily closes below a support level (or above a resistance level) before stopping out of positions. As discussed previously, the second close qualifies the move as a confirmed breakdown (or breakout) and helps me avoid whipsaws, which tend to stop out weak holders. Breakdowns and breakouts reflect a change in the balance between supply and demand, so we would not want to fight them and in some cases would even be comfortable taking the other side of the trade after being stopped out. The time when a percentage-based stop loss is appropriate is in parabolic uptrends and downtrends, where support and resistance are usually too far away to be a tolerable measure of risk.

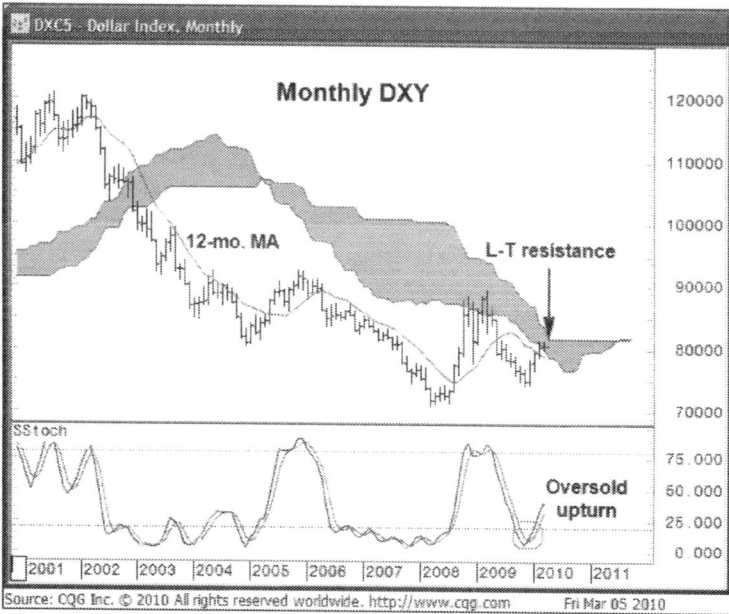

Figure 1: US dollar index at resistance level with Ichimoku

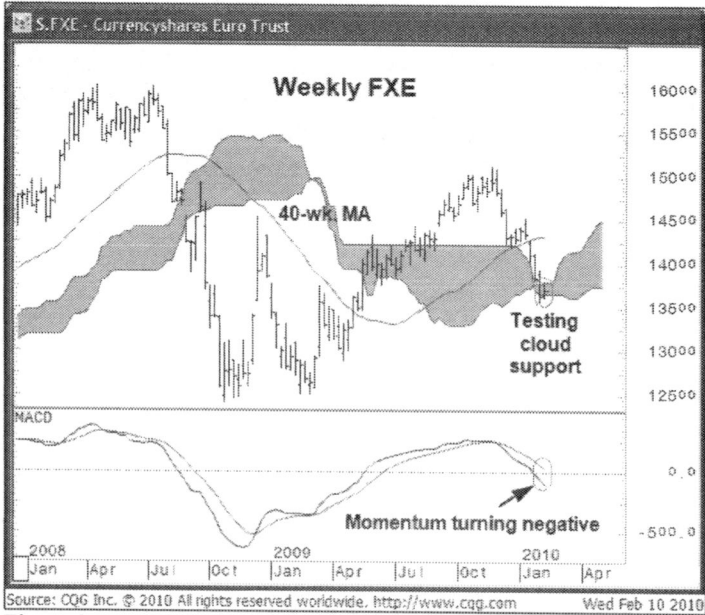

Figure 2: Measuring momentum with the MACD

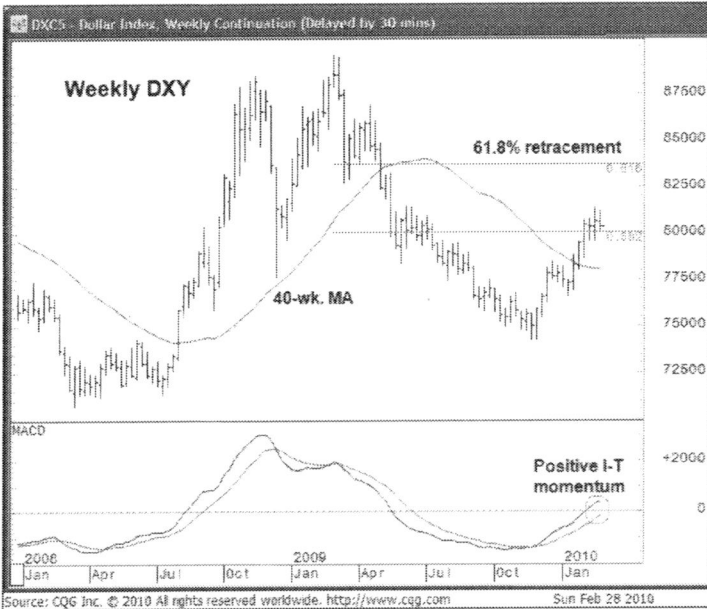

Figure 3: The 61.8% Fibonacci level

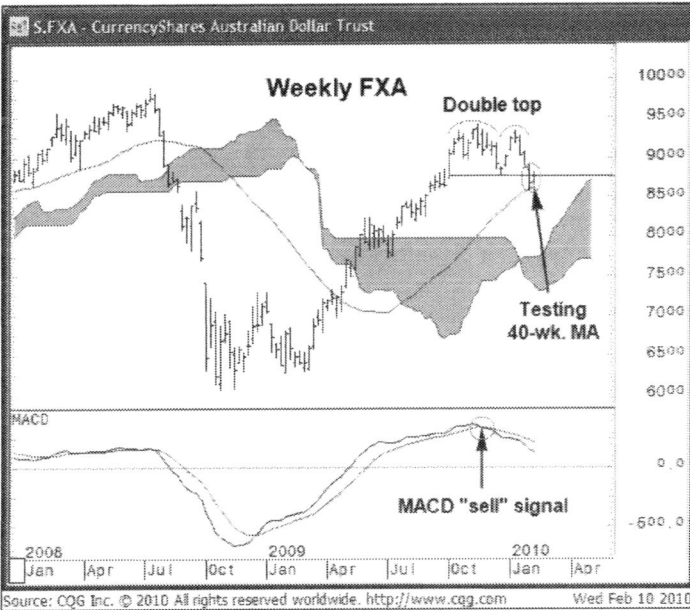

Figure 4: using the 40-week moving average

175

Chapter 12

GEOFF WILKINSON

HEAD OF INVESTMENT RESEARCH

MINT PARTNERS

Geoff Wilkinson has been head of investment research at Mint, a London-based independent trading house, for the last six years where he advises hedge funds and banks on trading strategies and investment decision making. Previously, Geoff held various proprietary trading roles within the international banking and asset management sectors.

USING TA FOR RESEARCH AND TRADING

Can you explain your basic research style?

The core approach is to identify as many 'tactical' investment opportunities as practical. By default, all trades must possess a well defined risk/reward ratio, one which incorporates a minimum of at least a '1' (risk) to '3' (reward) ratio from inception.

A 'tactical' focus aims to identify a profit potential (reward) of at least '5-10% per individual trading recommendation. 'Stop-losses' are an integral component. Subsequently, trailing stop-losses are incorporated to generate higher returns by running the 'winners' but this is not a mechanistic trailing process, but rather relies on independently identifying additional technical support or resistance levels en-route. Looking for 20% returns at the outset is a non-starter. Cash management gets you to 20%, not source material.

One essential facet of a tactical (short-term) process as opposed to a strategic (long-term) process is that it allows you to identify a significantly larger number of long and short investment propositions - an essential facet of any "long versus short 'balanced' portfolio" construction. Long-term returns, say a gain of 20% particularly in the equity markets, are invariably determined by 'beta'. As such your investment returns are invariably correlated and held hostage by the long-term trajectory of the equity market itself.

Finally, whilst some trades will aim to take advantage of potential reversal signals, the majority are trend friendly. Both traditional pattern analysis techniques and a proprietary quantitative directional momentum tool set are used to identify and calibrate trends.

Which markets do you cover?

The vast majority of the research in my current position is with equities. As such it covers the main markets but fully extends to cover currencies, commodities and fixed income as and when these markets and their components impinge and interact with equities.

How does your application of TA differ for short, medium and long-term time scales?

Apart from different time-frame charts, the techniques and analysis are almost entirely consistent. Investors collectively make the same decisions (fear and greed) regardless of the time-frame they are trading and it has never seemed intuitive to try and reinvent the wheel in this regard.

Do you think that the FX markets are more technically driven than other markets?

Together with the futures market, the FX Market is arguably and almost exclusively the most technically driven asset market. What is refreshing is that the equity market is in fact a lot more technical than it might initially appear, given that technical analysis is still a poor cousin from a traditional equity (valuation) research perspective. Increasingly though, it potentially takes a good bear market to reanimate interest (2007-2009); it is becoming a 'must have' rather than a peripheral skill-set where investment decision making is required.

How 'random' or efficient are the FX markets compared to the equity or fixed income markets?

To a large degree, the fact that you can trade the majority of currencies pairs and a great number of the minor ones on a 24 /7 basis facilitates the rapid and almost immediate discounting of news flow in the FX market. With the exception of the global bonds futures market, neither the volume nor the market access can compete with this in terms of efficiency.

To what extent are the FX markets driven by sentiment? Is this possible to quantify?

The FX market is entirely driven by prevailing investment sentiment rather than say economic fundamentals. Looking back over the last 20 years I have yet to be convinced, on a generic event driven basis, whether something as fundamental as a central bank cutting or increasing its interest rates will have a positive or negative affect on a currency going forward. In most cases the FX market will simply carry on with what it was doing before. Prevailing sentiment invariably translates into the strength of the underlying trend and this can be subjectively ascertained or objectively quantified.

What are the best sentiment indicators to use?

Trendlines and their relative slope (see Figure 1). From a quantitative perspective we have developed a proprietary tool to objectively grade prevailing trends (directional momentum) on a scale of +10 to -10 across all asset classes, including the major currency pairs.

INDICATORS AND STRATEGIES

Are there any indicators that work especially well in the FX markets?

I am generally not a huge fan of indicators as in most cases they are subtractive and all are derivatives of the underlying price action. Still, monitoring the RSI (overbought /oversold conditions) has merit, see Figure 2, and certainly has mass appeal and is widely followed. Volume however is a proverbial double edged sword and can be very ambiguous.

What is your reaction when the charts show a very obvious technical pattern such as a head-and-shoulders or a double top?

In contrast to the above, pattern analysis in tandem with trend analytics are an essential core component of my investment and trade

178

decision making process. In this regard the home truths of 'the devil is always in the detail' and 'history rhymes but never repeats itself' should always be borne in mind where pattern analysis is concerned. In this regard, head-and-shoulders trend reversal patterns can quite easily morph into triangular continuation patterns and often in fact do.

How do you indentify when a trend has commenced and may be nearing its end?

Traditional pattern analysis as noted above along with daily candlesticks patterns (key day reversals, bearish/bullish engulfing days) collectively combine with traditional trendline breaks to suggest an important shift in sentiment and a change in trend has or is transpiring. Subsequently this should be confirmed by a fundamental reversal in the residual pattern of investor buying and selling interest. In the event of a trend reversal one would expect to see a reversal in the prevailing series of significant highs and lows which define the trend. For example, a new low in a series of higher highs and higher lows which previously defined the uptrend.

Whilst an associated increase in volume can be a useful parameter to monitor in this regard, it is never the overriding consideration. As noted above, it can also be ambiguous. Markets can initially reverse on very low volumes, with volume levels improving subsequently. Often by then, the damage is done to your P&L.

Do you use Fibonacci, Gann or Elliott Wave techniques and if so, how?

I use both Elliott Wave and Fibonacci ratios frequently. In the case of the former, this dovetails fairly seamlessly with classic trend analysis and trend identification (Dow Theory). For the latter, Elliott Wave also potentially provides an intuitive framework to gauge the relationship between impulsive and corrective phases (the all important buyer / seller equilibrium – Figure 3).

There are important lessons to be learned early on in your career from being on the wrong side of a 'third wave'. Fibonacci retracement targets are also used and whilst the familiar ratios such as 50 %, 38.2% and 61.8% are all too frequently observed in practise to be ignored (Figure 4), the 76.4% 'last chance saloon' does occasionally enjoy its place in the sun. In general though, whilst Fibonacci ratios can be applied independently, they are particularly relevant when they coincide (and remarkably do seem to coincide) with other horizontal support and resistance levels, namely former significant highs and lows.

How do you use moving averages? If so, which periodicities do you use and do you use them directly to generate trade signals?

Whilst moving averages provide some input into our quantitative directional momentum tool set, they remain a relatively minor addition as far as my own TA research is concerned. Where they are consulted, I would look no further than the classic pairs.

It is always worth bearing in mind that moving averages by default are calculated from past data and contain no new information in that regard. They are consequently great at telling you what has happened 'on average' but there are better tools to employ if you want to look forward into the future.

If prices reach a major support level do you wait until it has broken through before buying or selling?

There are two considerations here. Firstly, the majority of my technical analysis is based on trendlines constructed on daily closing prices rather than on intraday prices. Whilst intraday prices clearly have their role to play, quite obviously if you are a day trader, it is the daily closing price which invariably crystallises everyone's P&L. They are simply more memorable and more relevant in terms of their psychological impact on support and resistance levels when broken. Once established they function very effectively on an intraday basis.

Secondly, there are no hard and fast rules where trendline breaks are concerned in terms of "by how much?" In my experience, simple rule applies; to the naked eye it has got to look like it has clearly broken. Whilst considerable care is needed when lining up the original closing prices to construct the trendline in the first place, if the break looks to be within the width of a proverbial pencil it isn't broken.

How do you judge if a market is overbought or oversold?

We would generally stick with a vanilla RSI reading as a first and only port of call. However, it is important to note that an 'oversold' indication is not necessarily just an indication of overzealous selling interest but could equally relate to a significant lack of buying interest as well. Extreme price movements are by definition a product of a severe mismatch between buying and selling interests in the market at that point in time. As a consequence, markets can crash when buying interest is further withdrawn and an 'oversold' indication can be easily become compounded into a severely 'oversold' one. Finally on the subject of the RSI, whilst this indicator is used primarily to identify potential turning points, it should be noted that there are also a great number of candlestick patterns (single and multiple days) which would also suggest that a degree of exhaustion is setting in.

CHARACTERISTICS UNIQUE TO THE FX MARKETS

What intraday effects impact the FX markets?
Obviously there is an intraday liquidity cycle, coincidental with the major market openings and closings in New York and London.

How far out do you analyze the FX markets? What specific strategies do you use for longer-term analysis?
For reasons outlined above and based on my previous experience there is very limited value in long-term FX analysis, since there are no reliable metrics which can deliver consistent monthly and quarterly returns. From a practical perspective, short-term trends can and do become medium-term trends which in turn can evolve into long-term trends, but it is potentially more productive to be able to identify when new short-term trends start and established trends finish.

Is there any difference in your approach between the analysis of G7 and emerging markets currencies? To what extent is liquidity in EM markets a factor?
There are no differences in the analytical methodologies applied between G7 and emerging markets currencies. However quite practical problems relate to execution and time localised liquidity constraints. As such your ability to hedge or cover positions outside opening hours can be severely constrained. This does not affect the analysis but is something that clearly needs to be addressed via the risk management process, particularly where cross currency portfolios are being considered. With the best will in the world it is not possible to effectively hedge one emerging market with another if they are not open for business at the same time.

181

To what extent do you look at fundamental information?

Not often since it is rarely relevant. Furthermore it is almost immediately discounted by the FX Market and as such has very little longevity going forward.

What fundamental information is most important for the FX markets?

An interesting question since the FX market, in spite of an innate ability to discount fundamental economic news flow and data almost immediately, does pay attention to it. The possible exception is unanticipated central bank intervention and even then the market has a gyroscopic ability to return to what it was doing before.

What is the best method of measuring volatility in the FX markets?

Measuring it historically is easy enough; predicting where it might be heading is clearly a lot more challenging. From previous experience correctly analysing historical price movements on an intraday basis (hourly data rather than daily data) and blending this with the market's own perception of risk (implied volatility) is potentially a good place to start.

Are the currency markets more or less prone to trending than stocks?

I have no particularly strong conviction on this and we haven't analysed it from a quantitative perspective. From an intuitive perspective both however demonstrate strong propensity to trend at all time scales and are both prone to mean reversion. Our quantitative 'directional momentum' analytical process objectively identifies developing and decaying trends in both.

Are there any specific currency pairs that are more prone to trending?

Historically anything against the yen was prone to trending but this was a product of the perception that persistent historical interest rate differentials at the time favoured a 'buy and hold' strategy and the so called 'carry trade' was born.

With interest rates now close to zero in all the major currencies over the last few years, one might have expected the propensity of currencies to trend to have diminished. Although you need to be quite careful about how you define a trend, this does not appear to have prevented the Swiss franc trending consistently stronger against the euro or the USD weakening consistently against the yen over the last few years. Quite possibly interest rate differentials had nothing to do with it originally, but as a guess most currencies can demonstrate a well defined propensity to exhibit trend.

Is it true that currencies are especially susceptible to market rumours? If so, why is this?

No; equities are more vulnerable particularly at the individual stock level. One aspect of the currency markets which is different from most other asset classes is that the cost of transacting in it remains remarkably low. Whilst there is very little transactional cost involved in jumping in with both feet on the back of a speculative rumour, the sheer amount of volume that needs to be transacted to capitalise on the rumour and keep the market moving in that direction is invariably substantial. Most rumours as far as the major currencies are concerned last only for a minute or two.

Is the carry trade still applicable for some currency pairs?

Potentially, but only where 'sufficient' and risk adjusted yield differentials exist, so not amongst the major currency pairs for the time being. Arguably the Australian dollar versus the Japanese yen seems like the most obvious (liquid) candidate. Still the relationship between yield differentials and a potential carry trade is unlikely to be linear. For example, below a certain threshold the incremental interest gain will be swamped by the intraday volatility in the particular currency. Conversely above a certain level in the case of a high yielding currency, investors who are not naïve will reach a point where the risk of holding that particular currency (devaluation) outweighs the perceived interest gain of holding it.

How is the impact on FX rates of the carry trade best measured?

For reasons outlined above this is potentially very hard to measure. The overall perception of the importance of the carry trade may outweigh the actual reality. The fact that the trend exists and looks likely to continue may provide a self-enforcing mechanism which helps to subsequently rationalise it.

Is it possible to differentiate between times when the market is being driven by speculators and by hedgers?

No; I would assume it's almost speculative certainly as far as the FX market is concerned. This has also become increasingly the case in commodities over the last few years.

How can intermarket analysis and cross asset correlations be used effectively when analysing currencies?

That has always been a very pertinent consideration but more money has been lost in the last 20 years by correlations breaking down than any other factor. Whilst there is money to be made by understanding the relationship between different asset classes it is almost certainly never a free lunch.

Do you keep an eye on volume levels and if so, how do you use them in your decisions? What is the best source of volume data for the FX markets?

We do not currently monitor volume levels in the FX market but do use it generically for trade confirmation in tandem with directional momentum. It can give very ambiguous and misleading signals at times

USING TA IN TRADING

Can you explain your approach to risk and money management?

Technical analysis is used comprehensively for risk management purposes in terms of timing all trade entry and exit points. These parameters are integral to the investment process and are set to meet stringent and consistent risk/reward parameters. Stop-losses are an integral component.

Stop-losses form an integral and core element of the investment and research analytical process. They are utilised in respect of well defined trendlines, typically constructed on a daily closing price basis. Since trend-lines by default represent equilibrium between buying and selling interests in the market at that particular point in time, a close above or below a trend-line implies that the previous equilibrium has changed. Put bluntly either the buyers or sellers have gained the upper hand and are now in the driving seat from a directional perspective. Furthermore, since the implicit risk/reward reverses when a trend-line is broken namely; sellers become forced buyers or vice versa and new risk/reward driven participants enter the market to take advantage of the change in the equilibrium, there is in fact quite transparently a valid mechanism underpinning the utilisation of stop-losses in a trading strategy.

Secondly, as noted previously there are no hard and fast rules where trend-line breaks are concerned in terms of "by how much?" In my experience, rather than get out the micrometer, a simple rule applies, principally; to the naked eye it has got to look like the trend-line has clearly broken. Whilst considerable care is mandated when lining up the original closing prices to construct the trend-line in the first place, if the break looks to be within the width of a proverbial pencil, it isn't broken.

How do you deal with false signals?

Even when great care is taken with individual trade selection, generating false signals is unavoidable. One useful filter which can help eliminate a lot of the intraday noise and false break signals is to simply construct trendlines based on the considerably more salient daily closing prices. Whilst to maintain consistency, 'Stop-loss' and 'Take profit' targets should follow this 'closing prices' lead, there is always a case for adding an intraday stop-loss overlay to prevent runaway losses developing.

Still 'false breaks' and subsequent reversals through well defined trend-lines can be very enlightening, since they are often a reliable indicator that the previous and prevailing investment sentiment in the direction of the expected and initial 'false' break has exhausted itself. Clearly this is very valuable information and if this can be married with a well defined risk/reward ratio, often the case since a major trend-line support or resistance is involved can form the basis of profitable trade in the opposite direction.

In fact, to reiterate an earlier point, it is invaluable to consider very carefully indeed what the market (investors) decided NOT to do, rather what they did do when confronted with an "obviously" profitable opportunity!

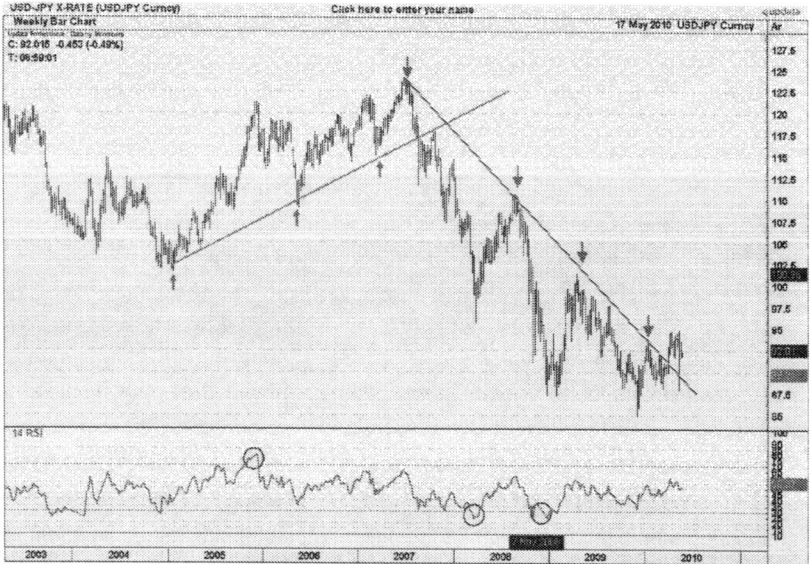

Figure 1: Up and down trend in USDJPY   Chart sources: Updata

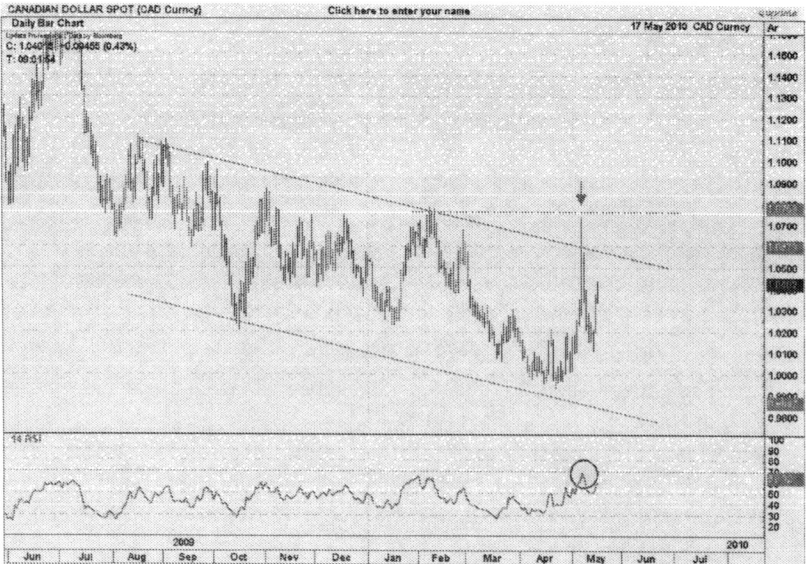

Figure 2: USDCAD RSI in overbought territory (selling opportunity)

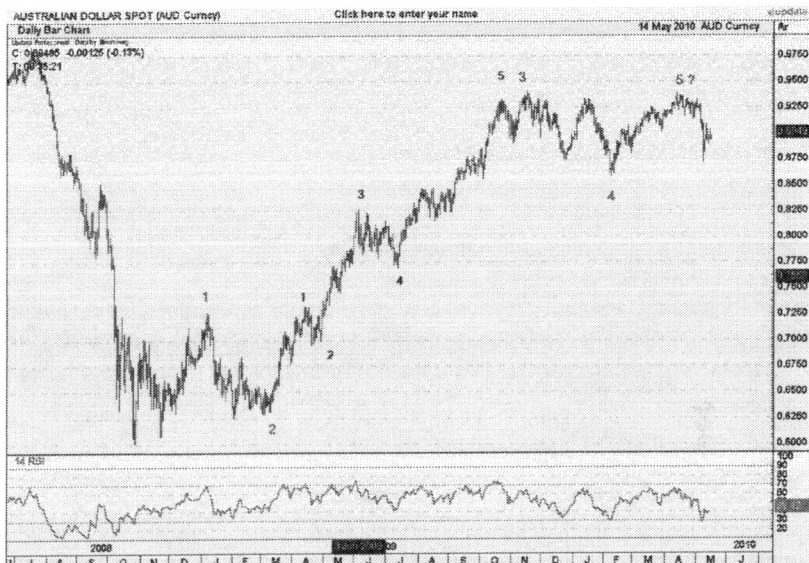

Figure 3: An Elliott Wave fractal wave count for AUSUSD

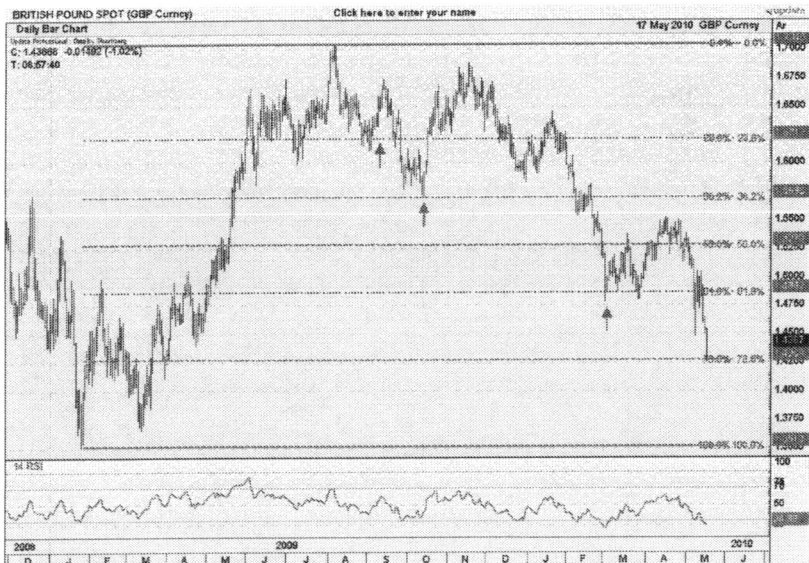

Figure 4: Fibonacci validating corrective levels for GBPUSD

Chapter 13

WALTER ZIMMERMANN

CHIEF TECHNCIAL ANALYST

UNITED-ICAP

Since 1995, Walter Zimmermann has served as Chief Technical Analyst for United-ICAP, formerly United Energy. He also served as the first Vice President and Chief Technical Analyst for petroleum with Lehman Brothers from 1988 to 1995. Prior to that, he worked as Vice President at E.F. Hutton and Amerex Petroleum.

USING TA FOR RESEARCH AND TRADING

Can you explain your basic research/trading style?

Our technical program is most concisely described as cycle-based pattern analysis. With cycle analysis as the foundation, our first floor of analysis consists of three main tools: classic chart pattern analysis using candlesticks, RSI momentum divergence, and sentiment divergence. Here we employ the "Bullish Consensus" service of Market Vane. Building on this level, the second floor is Elliott Wave analysis. It is on this level that we spend most of our time, effort and attention.

Which markets do you cover?

In currencies, we cover the Euro, the DX Index and the Canadian dollar. We also cover equities, metals and crude oil.

Do you think that the FX markets are more technically driven than other markets?

Based on almost thirty years of continual analysis it is our contention that fundamental news always follows the price action, and in every market. Our experience has convinced us beyond a shadow of doubt that the dynamics that drive price trends in all market are endogenous, not exogenous. In other words, what appear as fundamental developments are actually delayed attempts to rationalize a price trend reversal that has already happened. The news follows the trend, always and especially in the FX.

How 'random' or efficient are the FX markets compared to the equity or fixed income markets?

'Random' and 'efficient' are not related terms. They are two different, but extremely important issues. So, we prefer to deal with them separately. A random market is one where the next trade is not related to the previous trade. And one thing the market is not is a random number generator. The ubiquity of fractal price patterns and the omnipresent Fibonacci ratio retracements tells us that in the FX markets, the next trade is a function of the previous. There are price trends and peaking and bottoming patterns. I suspect that the issue of randomness emerged as an artifact of academic types repeatedly getting short into major market lows and long into major peaks.

The issue of efficiency relates to how quickly and completely new information is translated into price adjustments. In this regard, we find that the currency markets are especially inefficient. For example, on December 4, 2009 we got a long-term DX Index buy signal from a 75.91 close (Figure 1) that targeted a multi-month advance. For the next few months, the major investment banks issued a steady stream of losing short trade recommendations on the DX Index. They each were stopped out one-by-one. Their extremely bearish sentiment had blinded them to the risks of higher prices ahead. In fact, to their eyes the US dollar fundamentals did not start to improve until March and by then the DX had already reached the 81.000 area.

The shorts got married to their positions. They were thereby rendered oblivious to the fact that the US dollar was oversold. They were blinded to the deeply serious problems unfolding for the Euro. One cannot act on information if one is blind to it.

One cannot discount information if one is in denial. It has been our experience that this 'living in denial' factor is what makes currency trends more enduring than trends in any other market. About half of an up trend in currencies is driven by bears treating the rally as an opportunity to add to their short position. Halfway into the trend they give up and then start citing pre-existing news as justification for finally getting long. This is not an efficient market.

Why is this denial element so strong in currencies? In other words, why does new information seem to take so long to be discounted in currencies? We think the answer relates to the illusion that each country is in control of its own currency. The inexperienced tend to believe government announcements, forecasts and intentions at face value. The fact is: no nation has sovereignty over its own currency. The markets are the only sovereign power here.

To what extent are the FX markets driven by sentiment? Is this possible to quantify?

Sentiment plays an enormous role in the FX markets. Into major market peaks you find extremely bullish sentiment readings and into major lows you find extremely bearish sentiment readings. In fact, it is these sentiment extremes that make the trend so enduring once it reverses. However, as with any other tool, a sentiment index must be handled properly. One must know the entire sentiment history so the over-bullish and over-bearish extremes can be identified in real time. And it has been our experience that one must seek out the sentiment divergence that helps confirm trend reversals: new lows in price unaccompanied by a more bearish sentiment extreme, or new highs in price that lack an even more bullish sentiment reading.

There are technical tools that attempt to quantify sentiment and, as with any category of technical tools, some sentiment tools are more useful than others. We rate some sentiment indicators as too jittery. They tend to reach extreme readings too early on into the trend. We like the **Market Vane** service (Figure 2). However, in a very real sense, all technical indicators are sentiment indicators. For example, what is a major candlestick reversal pattern on a monthly chart other than a sentiment reversal indicator? And what is a major RSI divergence other than an indication of the exhaustion of a sentiment extreme (Figures 3 and 4)? And what is a completed five wave pattern in Elliott Wave (Figure 5) other than an indication that the sentiment has completely reversed from one sentiment extreme to the other?

Are there any market conditions under which TA works better or worse than other times?

This is an extremely important question to ask. If you do a close study of bottoming and peaking action into major trend reversals, you will find an astonishing fact; no down trend has ever ended with a bullish surprise. Down trends never end with an unexpected bullish development. Similarly, no up trend has ever ended with a bearish surprise.

First, let us cover peaking action. To the inexperienced it seems logical that an up trend would end on bearish news. However, the markets are not logical and no up trend has ever ended with a bearish news story. In fact, into the later stages of a longer-term uptrend the news is only bullish. Any bearish development is never covered. It is after all an uptrend, so reporting a bearish development is not just irrelevant, it will never make it past the editor. And the longer the uptrend persists, the more bullish the news must be in order to be deemed relevant. In every case, for every market and for every trend **we have followed in the last thirty years, an uptrend ends when a news story, more bullish than any previously reported, fails to sustain the up trend.**

The bulls are first confused, then alarmed."Well if that story could not rally the markets, then why am I still long?" The alarm is eventually followed by sell orders. Sell stops trigger other sell stops, and all from a bullish news story.

On the day the market fails to respond to that even more bullish story, technicians will likely be getting bearish RSI divergence, bearish sentiment divergence, bearish candlestick reversal patterns and, in all likelihood, evidence for a major wave count completion to the upside. Fundamental analysts are buffaloed and call it an overdue correction. Technicians are delighted with the range of confirming indications of a major trend reversal.

It is the same story at major lows. No downtrend has ever ended with a surprise bullish development. In fact, into the later stages of a longer-term down trend the news is only bearish. The longer the downtrend has persisted, the more bearish the news must be in order to be deemed relevant. In every trend we have followed in the last thirty years, downtrends end when a news story more bearish than any so far proves unable to sustain the decline.

The bears are first confused then alarmed: "Well if that extremely bearish development could not sustain the decline, then why am I still short?" If after a couple weeks the down trend has still failed to resume, the consternation of the bears generates buy orders to exit the shorts. Buy stops trigger other buy stops and all from an extremely bearish news story.

When the sentiment extreme finally exhausts itself no amount of fundamental news can keep the trend going. A good technical system will get a trend reversal signal early on. Meanwhile the fundamental analysts invariably shift into denial mode: "It is just an overdue correction." They will advise scale up selling from major lows or scale down buying from a major peak. This living in denial will ensure the trend persists. Our experience tells us that technical analysis shines the brightest at major bottoming and peaking action.

INDICATORS AND STRATEGIES

Are there any indicators that work especially well in the FX markets?

I vividly remember the first time I did a wave count analysis of a currency. I had been covering equity indices and the energy sector for a few years. A client who had more exposure to the Japanese Yen than to jet fuel asked me for a wave count analysis of the Yen. The best way I can describe the experience was that it was as if I had been walking into the wind for five years and suddenly the wind stopped. Of all the sectors that we cover, we still find that the principles of Elliott Wave analysis are most perfectly expressed in the various currency markets. In fact, to this day, whenever a client tells us that they want to learn Elliott Wave analysis we urge them to start with a currency.

What is your reaction when the charts show a very obvious technical pattern such as a head-and-shoulders or a double top?

Classic chart patterns, like the head-and-shoulders, develop over time. They do not suddenly appear one day. So, as an unfolding classical chart pattern enters its final stage, we are looking for confirming indicators like momentum and sentiment divergence and candlestick reversal patterns. We are much more aggressive if there is confirmation across a range of indicators. Without such confirmation, we remain in a 'wait and see' mode.

What are the most reliable candlestick reversal patterns?

The real issue here is not so much the type of candlestick pattern, but whether the intensity of the trend reversal is expected to be mild or wild. To gauge how dramatic the candlestick reversal pattern is likely to be when it does finally occur we look to three factors:

1. The duration of the trend that is about to end.
2. How overbought or oversold the market is in momentum terms.
3. How overdone the market is in sentiment terms.

The more enduring and overdone the trend, the more likely the candlestick reversal pattern will be both dramatic and unmistakable. The other point that must be made here is that a weekly candlestick reversal pattern is much more significant than a daily reversal and a monthly candle reversal is much more significant than a weekly reversal.

How do you identify when a trend has commenced and may be nearing its end?
For us the ideal bottoming and/or peaking signal consists of three key factors, listed in order of importance:

1. A major scale wave count pattern completion

2. Candlestick reversal patterns on daily and weekly charts

3. RSI and ideally sentiment divergence as well

What is the best method for measuring price momentum in the market?
Call us old fashioned, but we are big fans of the simple, old 14-day RSI. For our purposes, trading the intermediate to longer-term trends, we find the stochastic tends to be too jittery and thereby give overbought and oversold signals way too early.

Do you use Fibonacci, Gann or Elliott Wave techniques and if so, how?
We employ Elliott Wave and Fibonacci ratio analysis extensively on spot continuation charts. In fact, we spent most of our day fine-tuning our various wave count models.

Which Fibonacci ratios are most reliable and why?

It is quite easy to calculate Fibonacci ratios without any reference to an Elliott wave analysis. However, this approach can give the mistaken notion that any degree of ratio retracement or ratio multiple is equally likely at any one time. This is of course entirely untrue. The probability of a retracement holding a specific Fibonacci ratio is completely a function of where the price pattern is in the larger wave count. For examples:

- The wave 'four' following an extended wave 'three' should not retrace more than .236 of the wave 'three.'
- The typical retracement for a 'B' wave is .618 of the 'A.'
- In the higher volatility markets a wave 'two' is most likely to retrace near to .7862 of the wave 'one.'

How do you establish price targets using Elliott Wave analysis and Fibonacci?

The first point to emphasize here is that the highest probability ratio retracement is always a function of the phase of the wave pattern. If one's wave count model is incorrect then it will likely require pure coincidence to correctly forecasting the actual Fib ratio.

With regard to forecasting price targets using Elliott Wave, there is no short answer. The first tip is to always begin a wave count analysis of a new market with the big picture. We always start with a price chart that ideally goes back to day one of trading in that particular market. Beginning a wave count analysis with a ninety-day chart is asking for trouble as it will leave you utterly clueless as to where you are in the larger Elliott Wave pattern. Your P&L is at great risk without this knowledge.

The second tip is to avoid only having one wave count model. In this regard, we have found it very helpful over the years to always have an alternate model. If this key support breaks then the main count is voided and this alternate count becomes the highest probability outcome.

EW is often criticized for being too subjective and for being difficult to identify when a wave starts/finishes. How do you overcome this?

Based on almost thirty years of continuous experience, it is our contention that no one technical tool is an effective, stand-alone, self-sufficient system. We view the multiple systems approach as an

194

indispensable requirement, not as over-analysis. The question here is one we first faced back in the early 1980's. Is there a way to "cheat" at Elliott Wave analysis? Are there other technical tools that assist in the task of identifying major wave pattern completions?

As we began our analysis of the markets with energy futures, our first step was to identify consistent seasonal price cycles. We also employ RSI divergence, sentiment divergence and, of course, candlestick analysis. We would not even consider attempting a wave count analysis without the benefit of these additional tools.

How do you use moving averages? If so, which periodicity do you use and do you use them directly to generate trade signals?

It has been our experience that major equity indices like the S&P500 are the only place where a moving average cross system is of any value. A moving average is very much a lagging indicator. Our clients demand to know when a trend is reversing in real time. They do not want to hear that a trend reversed six weeks ago and the moving average is only just now confirming that. In fact, we call moving averages 'the Hostess Twinkies' of technical analysis. They are fun and colorful, but offer no nutritional value.

If prices reach a major support level do you wait until it has broken through before buying or selling?

If a market declines into a major support level, we prefer to wait for the shape of the daily candlestick. Given the higher volatility that tends to accompany major tops and bottoms we often find that a market can spend most of the day below our key support level only to surge higher at the end of the day into a bullish hammer bottom with bullish RSI divergence that closes well above the key support. The aim here is to avoid being stopped out by the volatility of bottoming and peaking action.

How do you judge if a market is overbought or oversold?

For our purposes, we need to see actual RSI (Relative Strength Index) divergence. It is not enough for us to have a very high or a very low RSI reading. We need to see divergence - either new highs in the price unaccompanied by new highs in the RSI or new lows in the price unaccompanied by new lows in the RSI.

CHARACTERISTICS UNIQUE TO THE FX MARKETS

What intraday effects impact the FX markets?

Our focus is the intermediate to longer-term currency trends. Intra-day we are more concerned with the effects of FX market moves on the commodity markets, specifically the cause and effect relationship between the DX Index (cause) and crude oil prices (effect). It is our contention that intra-day FX responses to transient news events are not trend reversal capable.

How far out do you analyse the FX markets? What specific strategies do you use for longer-term analysis?

It has been our experience that a carefully done, objective Elliott Wave analysis is completely capable of forecasting multi-year trends and of predicting multi-year trend target zones (Figures 6 and 7).

Is there any difference in your approach between the analysis of G7 and emerging markets currencies? To what extent is liquidity in EM markets a factor?

Our principle FX market coverage includes the DX Index, the Euro, the Canadian dollar and the Japanese Yen. Over the years, we have seen a direct relationship between the clarity and precision of the Elliott Wave patterns and the liquidity of the market. This is the case for both outright currencies and currency pairs. Fortunately, the FX markets that our clients want us to cover are also the most liquid.

To what extent do you look at fundamental information?

As technicians the only value we see in new fundamental information is the price response. A true bull market will routinely ignore bearish news while a bear market will consistently ignore bullish news. A related phenomenon is the ancient proverb 'the news follows the trend.' The wisdom of this proverb is regularly visible and critically significant in major trend reversals (Figure 8).

At major lows, both the news and the fundamentals that the market deems relevant are always and only bearish. From a major reversal higher it can take weeks or even months before the 'fundamentals' begin to improve. This phenomenon was especially clear into the DX Index lows of both March 2008 and November 2009.

Similarly, the fundamentals into a major peak are always bullish. As we have previously noted, it is when a bull market fails to continue to advance on 'improving fundamentals' that we get interested. And it is when a bear market fails to continue lower on 'worsening fundamentals' that we shift to high alert for bottoming action.

What is the best method of measuring volatility in the FX markets?

We find an accurate Elliott Wave model to be the best predictor of trends in volatility. Specific phases of both five wave and 'ABC' type patterns have a characteristic volatility profile when compared to adjacent phases. While even the most precisely accurate wave count pattern cannot predict precise volatility levels, our system does not require that type of information. We measure our success by our ability to anticipate the duration and extent of price trends. If we get that right, then volatility takes care of itself. If we get that wrong, then no amount of volatility measurement will correct the situation.

Are the currency markets more or less prone to trending than stocks?

It has been our longstanding experience that nothing trends as well or as clearly as a major currency market - not equity indices, not commodity markets and not even long term treasuries.

What determines the 'key levels' in the FX markets?

As technicians, we feel compelled to emphasize that the critical pivot prices for trends in currency values are a function of the price patterns in the market. Because the trend creates the news and because the trend determines which fundamentals are relevant, relying on exogenous factors to determine key levels is to employ lagging indicators, not leading or even coincident indicators.

To what extent are FX markets seasonal? Can you give some examples of seasonality in currencies?

As I have already mentioned, we look at market cycles. Our focus is on the following:

- Economic scale time cycles - On this scale the principle cycle is the Kondratieff Wave (Figure 9). Our understanding of the sixty-year long (plus or minus) Kondratieff Wave is that it is a generational scale Hyman Minsky debt cycle. The bursting of the credit bubble into 2005 was forecast by another level cycle.

- Investment scale time cycles - The principle cycle for us on this scale is an eighteen-year real estate cycle that was due to peak into 2005. This cycle takes eighteen years to complete - that is nine years up and then nine years down. We also track two commodity cycles, a thirteen year and an eight year.

- Seasonal cycles - We are big fans of seasonality and have done a great deal of work calculating 25 year average seasonal cycles for the various markets. Obviously, energy prices are intensely seasonal, but then so is the stock market, the US dollar and treasuries.

We have done many years of research into seasonal influences in the major markets both financial and nonfinancial. It is our conclusion that seasonal trends are grossly underutilized. The strict quantitative approach seems to be especially dismissive of seasonal influences and, of course, there is no room for a seasonal cycle in the 'efficient market hypothesis.' For us, this is just as well. The more the financial community dismisses seasonal timing cues, the longer those factors will continue to be tradeable. One example of seasonality in the currency markets is the tradition of spring lows in the DX Index (Figures 10-12).

How do you measure the impact that fund flows have on specific currencies?

For those who manage to be successful at forecasting currency trend reversals, fund flow information is a lagging indicator. For those not employing technical analysis, fund flow information is probably worth its weight in gold. We rate fund flow information as perhaps analogous to a 100-day moving average. It tells you that the trend has already reversed some time ago. In Elliott Wave terms, we see fund flows as a factor that typically drives the 'third wave extension,' the phase that occurs well after waves 'one' and 'two' have finished. By then the low hanging fruit is already gone and volatility is already shooting higher.

Is it true that currencies are especially susceptible to markets rumors? If so, why is this?

If moving averages are the 'Hostess Twinkies' of technical analysis, then rumors are the 'Hostess Cupcakes' of fundamental analysis. Like 'Hostess Cupcakes,' rumors are colorful and delicious. However, just like Hostess Cupcakes, market rumors give only a short buzz and are completely lacking in nutritional value. Rumors are never the stuff of major trend reversals. They often accompany short-term corrections, but, even in this case, it has been our experience that rumors arise as an effort to explain an unanticipated price move.

Is the carry trade still applicable for some currency pairs?

We view the whole concept of a carry trade as the aftermath of the euphoria phase of Hyman Minsky's debt cycle. It is the use of borrowed money to pursue highly leveraged speculative trades. We are confident that Minsky would rate the carry trade as 'Ponzi borrowing.'

The basic requirement for a carry trade is a dramatic and persistent interest rate differential across a currency pair. Such differentials are very unlikely in a global bull market. However, following the 'euphoria phase' a global bull market will begin to come undone at different speeds in different countries, thereby creating dramatic interest rate differentials. So we see the carry trade as characteristic of a specific phase in the financial cycle of the global economy.

How is the impact on FX rates of the carry trade best measured?

We think this question is asking how to best measure the impact of the interest rate differential of the currency pair at the heart of a carry trade. Recent history suggests that this impact can only be accurately measured once the carry trade is broken. For example, it was only after the Yen carry trade broke that it became clear how many markets had been bid up to unsustainable levels through the leverage made available by this carry trade.

Is it possible to differentiate between markets driven by speculators as opposed to by hedgers?

199

This issue is simple to track in a market like crude oil where the CFTC Commitment of Traders (COT) covers a broad swath of market volume. However, it has been our experience that tracking the relative participation of hedgers and speculators does not help us to forecast either the duration or extent of price trends.

This question reminds me of one that was frequently asked in the early days down on the NYMEX trading floor. Clients would regularly ask, "Who is buying" and "who is selling?" It is our contention that if one were able to answer such questions it would only give one a false sense of security. One would thereby have facts with no bearing on the extent or duration of the trend.

However, we do think that insight into this issue can help one understand market dynamics. In WTI crude oil, our research has found that, in general, the longer an uptrend persists the more bullish the producers get. The more bullish producers become, the more they tend to reduce the size of their short hedge. So by the time a longer-term up trend peaks out, the producers have near maximum exposure to lower prices. And the longer a downtrend in crude persists, the more bearish refineries get and the smaller becomes their long hedge position. So by the time a longer-term down trend has bottomed out, refiners tend to have near maximum exposure to higher prices.

A dramatic instance of this dynamic was recently observed in gold. Within a few weeks of a multi-decade peak in the price of gold, Barrick announced they were going to spend billions of dollars to buy back all their short hedges. And these billions of dollars were being raised through a massive dilution of shareholder equity. While this program was announced back in September 2009, the shares of Barrick have yet to recover despite a continuing up trend in the price of gold.

Human nature being what it is, we suspect that if one is really intent on finding whether a currency is being driven by hedgers or speculators, it would be wise to look for the contrarian influence that we have repeatedly seen in crude and that was recently visible for all to see in the instance of Barrick gold.

Do you keep an eye on volume levels and if so, how do you use them in your decisions? What is the best source of volume data for the FX markets?

We see the difficulties in gathering volume data in currency trends as next to insurmountable. Given the sheer size of the FX market, the

200

depth and range of the players and the geographical sweep of the centers of FX trading, finding the Holy Grail seems an easier task than gathering FX volumes. The value of such information would be clear. In both equities and commodities, the volume still 'goes with the trend.' However, we suggest that there is an alternate approach. It is our view that a daily sentiment indicator is a much more useful tool than daily volume.

Is TA a part of your risk assessment? For example, do you use support and resistance as likely levels to which the market will head?

Our on-going price risk assessment is 100% technical analysis. All of our support and resistance points, price targets and trend duration indications are entirely technical based.

What impact did the turmoil in 2008 have on your returns? What action have you taken to reduce losses?

From December 2007 into June 2008, we recommended a few critical trades to our subscribers in currencies. Across Q1 of 2008, we recommended a scale down buy in the DX index into the 73.40 to 67.50 zone, targeting a multi-year advance to the 93.00 area. We were not able to complete that scale down buy as the 67.500 was never reached. However, the 93.00 area is still our upside target.

Figure 1: Long-term buy signal for US Dollar Index on 2/19/09

Figure 2: The Market Vane sentiment indicator

Figure 3: RSI divergence

Figure 4: Sentiment divergence

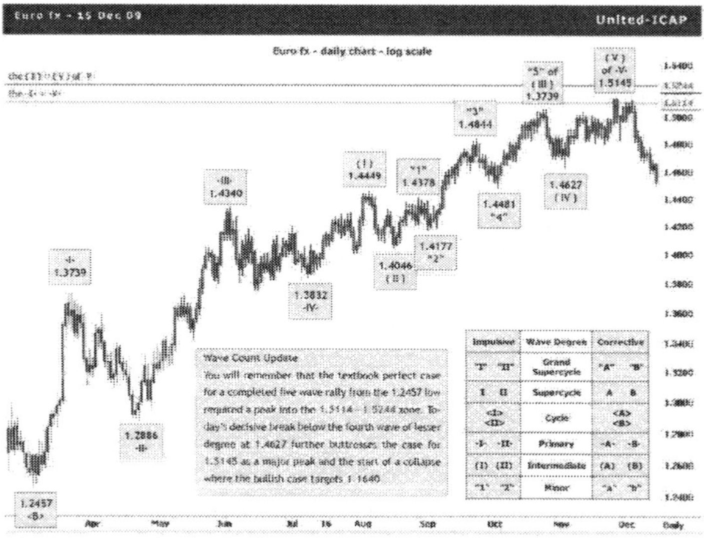

Figure 5: 5-wave Elliott Wave pattern

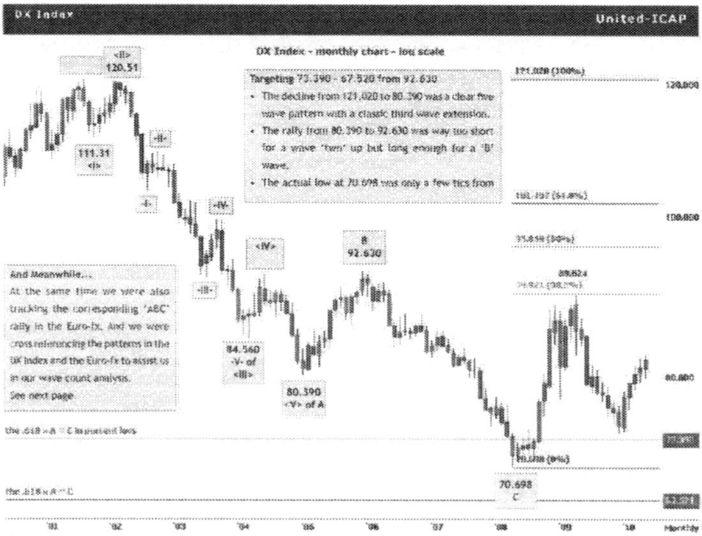

Figure 6: Elliott Wave and multi-year trends in the US dollar index

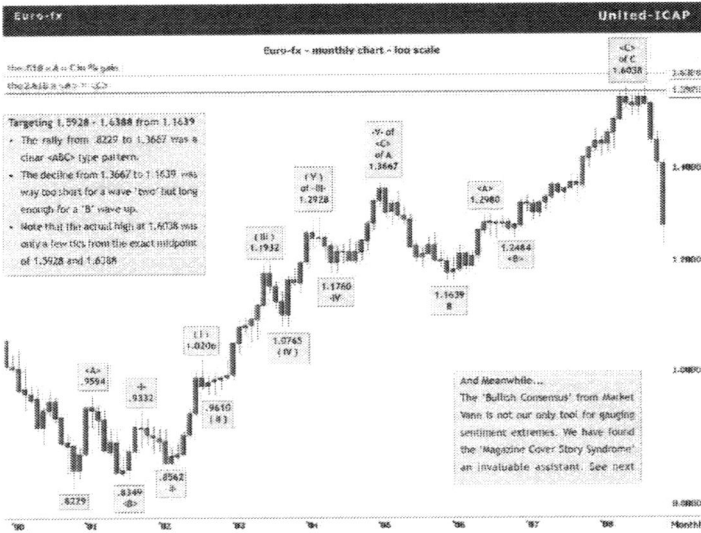

Figure 7: Elliott Wave and multi-year trends in the Euro

Figure 8: News follows the trend

205

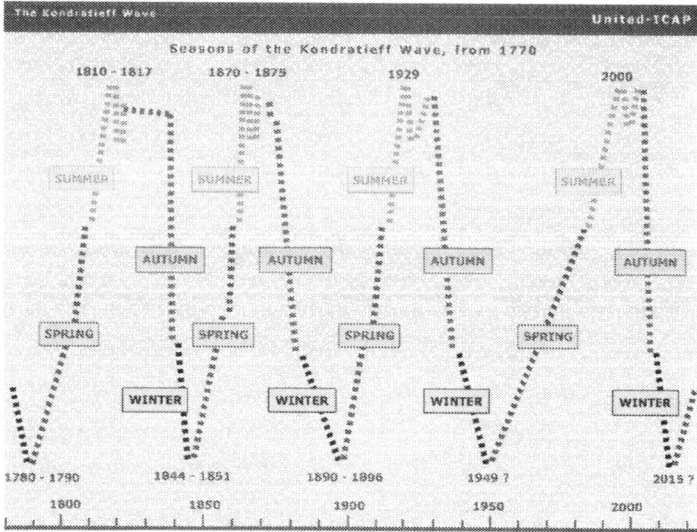

Figure 9: The Kondratieff Wave and seasonality

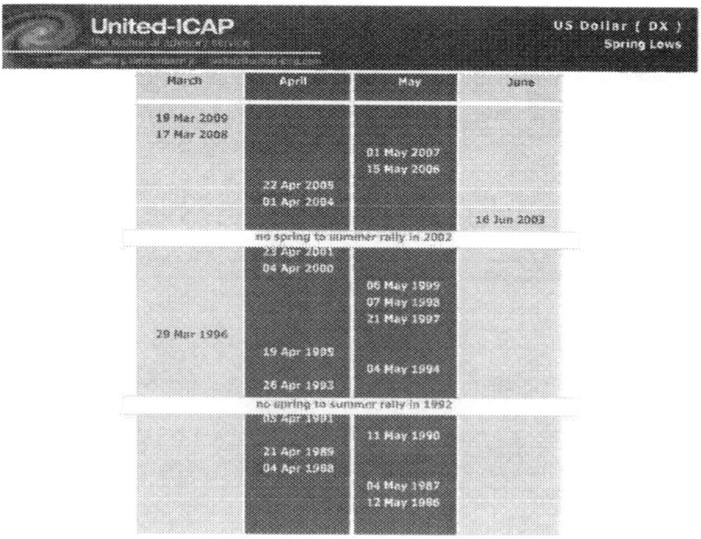

Figure 10: Spring/summer seasonality in the US dollar index

United-ICAP — US Dollar (DX) Ensuing Highs

Apr - May	Jun	Jul	Aug	Sep	Oct - Nov
20 Apr 2009					21 Nov 2008
	13 Jun 2007				
		19 Jul 2006			
		08 Jul 2005			
			26 Aug 2003		
no spring rally in 2002					
	06 Jul 2001				26 Oct 2000
		12 Jul 1999			
			17 Aug 1998		
			06 Aug 1997		
28 May 1996				14 Sep 1995	
			02 Aug 1993		
no spring rally in 1992					
		02 Jul 1991			
	04 Jun 1990				
	15 Jun 1969				
			22 Aug 1988		
			11 Aug 1987		
	02 Jun 1986				

Figure 11: Spring/summer seasonality in the US dollar index

United-ICAP — US Dollar (DX) Spring to Summer Rallies

Low Date	Low	% Bulls	Peak Date	High	% Bulls	% Gain
19 Mar 2009	82.631	58%	20 Apr 2009	86.871	68%	5.1%
17 Mar 2008	70.698	16%	21 Nov 2008	88.463	81%	25.1%
01 May 2007	81.251	28%	13 Jun 2007	83.272	34%	2.5%
15 May 2006	83.600	39%	19 Jul 2006	87.330	43%	4.5%
22 Apr 2005	83.360	32%	08 Jul 2005	90.770	54%	8.9%
01 Apr 2004	87.020	38%	14 May 2004	92.250	43%	6.0%
16 Jun 2003	91.880	18%	26 Aug 2003	99.490	46%	8.3%
23 Apr 2001	113.86	79%	06 Jul 2001	121.020	82%	6.3%
04 Apr 2000	104.25	77%	26 Oct 2000	119.070	95%	14.2%
06 May 1999	99.390	68%	12 Jul 1999	104.880	96%	5.5%
07 May 1998	98.970	49%	17 Aug 1998	102.880	88%	4.4%
21 May 1997	93.070	47%	06 Aug 1997	101.790	92%	9.4%
29 Mar 1996	86.100	45%	28 May 1996	89.040	83%	3.4%
19 Apr 1995	80.050	11%	14 Sep 1995	87.470	80%	9.3%
04 May 1994	91.510	28%	06 Jun 1994	93.580	40%	2.3%
		25%	02 Aug 1993	95.800	62%	8.4%
26 Apr 1993	88.370					
05 Apr 1991	89.290		02 Jul 1991	97.320		9.0%
11 May 1990	90.660		04 Jun 1990	93.360		3.0%
21 Apr 1989	96.190		15 Jun 1989	103.99		8.1%
04 Apr 1988	87.870		22 Aug 1988	99.510		13.4%
04 May 1987	94.820		11 Aug 1987	101.740		7.3%
12 May 1986	110.900		02 Jun 1986	118.03		6.8%

Average Gains

For the ten years 2000 to 2009 the average rally from the spring low has been gain in value of 8.7%.

For all years listed here the average gain is 7.8%

Remember we are talking about swings in the value of the world's reserve currency here, not something wild and crazy like Gasoline. These are impressive gains for any currency.

Figure 12: Spring/summer seasonality in the US dollar index

INDEX